In some parts of the country there is a co-op level not ....
since the 1930s. *Cooperation Works!* describes these new types
of cooperatives and their role in solving both urban and rural
problems.

Charles Snyder, President
National Cooperative Bank

Cooperation Works! tells of the success stories of new types
of cooperatives emerging to meet the changing needs of rural
America.

Richard Rominger, Deputy Secretary of Agriculture,
U.S. Department of Agriculture, Washington, D.C.

The key to sustainability and growth opportunities for rural
communities is the development of partnerships where businesses,
local governments, key community leaders, agricultural producers
and elected officials pool their resources and pursue common
goals– especially across community boundaries.

Kathy Beery, Division Administrator
Iowa Department of Economic Development

Cooperation Works! highlights successful cooperative
projects across a broad spectrum of American society and
introduces creative ideas for implementation. Cooperative leaders
will find *Cooperation Works!* enlightening and stimulating
reading.

Tom Lyon, CEO, Cooperative Resources International
President, National Cooperative Business Association

Long ago, farmers organized cooperatively to control the cost
of their feed, seed and supplies and to improve their bargaining
power over the sale price of their products. Since then,
cooperatives have formed in many other sectors, providing
millions of people with better access to essential goods and
services. I expect the role of cooperatives will become even more
important in the coming years.

Russ Feingold, U.S. Senator, Wisconsin

ACKNOWLEDGMENTS

As one might expect from a book on cooperation, many supportive and committed individuals and organizations made this endeavor possible. More than anyone else, Jim Arts, the Executive Director of Cooperative Development Services (CDS) deserves our gratitude for his insightful editing, encouragement and leadership as the book moved from a rough idea to a finished product. Dianne Molvig did an excellent job as editor, crafting our individual styles and chapters into a consistent and readable outcome. Mary Myers of CDS provided valuable comments on nearly every chapter. The staff members at CDS have all added value at every step of the way.

Because each chapter is about a distinctive form of cooperation we wished to show our gratitude to the almost one hundred people who guided the overall book. Therefore, after each chapter we acknowledge those who provided case study and chapter-specific information or who reviewed chapter drafts.

A project like this takes time and money. We are especially grateful for the financial support and friendly advice we received from William Nelson, Executive Director of The Cooperative Foundation. In particular, we would like to thank the following for their critical support without which this book would not have been possible; MSI Insurance Foundation, Nationwide Insurance Enterprise Foundation, The Cooperative Foundation, the Cooperative Development Foundation, and the Center for Cooperative at University of California, Davis. We commend them for championing cooperative enterprises.

Last, but certainly not least, a book on cooperation could not be written without the support and understanding of our work mates, friends and families. Thanks in particular go to Isaac and Luc Nadeau, Brady Wright and the rest of the Nadeau family and to Ann Evans, Hatley Rose and the rest of the Evans Thompson families.

While acknowledging the critically important help of all of these people and organizations, the authors take full responsibility for the content of Cooperation Works!, including any factual errors it may contain.

We are grateful to those readers and cooperators who believe that "cooperation works" and hope that many more enterprises are inspired by the models presented in our book.

E.G. Nadeau
David J. Thompson

Dear Robb —
Best Wishes
David
Let's do more!

COOPERATION WORKS!
How People Are Using Cooperative Action
to Rebuild Communities and Revitalize the Economy

E. G. NADEAU
&
DAVID J. THOMPSON

LONE OAK PRESS, LTD.

COOPERATION WORKS!
How People Are Using Cooperative Action
to Rebuild Communities and Revitalize the Economy

BY
E. G. NADEAU & DAVID J. THOMPSON

PUBLISHED
BY
LONE OAK PRESS, LTD.
304 11TH AVENUE SOUTHEAST
ROCHESTER, MINNESOTA 55904
507-280-6557

First Edition
ISBN NUMBER 1-883477-13-1
LIBRARY OF CONGRESS CARD CATALOG NUMBER 96-78132

COVER PHOTO BY E. G. NADEAU
The colors in the cover picture represent the
colors of the rainbow, a symbol of cooperation.

SPONSORED BY COOPERATIVE DEVELOPMENT SERVICES

Cooperative Development Services (CDS) coordinated the preparation and publication of Cooperation Works!

CDS is a non-profit organization that provides professional business development and planning services to cooperatives and communities in the Upper Midwest.

Since its start in 1985, CDS has conducted hundreds of cooperative, community and economic development projects in areas as diverse as agriculture, business, the environment, housing, child care, and the arts.

For further information contact:

Cooperative Development Services
30 W. Mifflin St., Suite 401
Madison, WI 53703
608-258-4396

Financial support for the book provided by:

MSI INSURANCE FOUNDATION

NATIONWIDE INSURANCE ENTERPRISE FOUNDATION

COOPERATIVE DEVELOPMENT FOUNDATION

THE COOPERATIVE FOUNDATION

CENTER FOR COOPERATIVES, UNIVERSITY OF CALIFORNIA-DAVIS

COOPERATION WORKS!

Contents

FOREWORD

The tradition of democratic economic enterprise reaches far back into American history. Formally organized cooperatives, such as mutual fire insurance societies, date back to colonial times. Informal cooperative action pervades our early history in the form of barn raisings, threshing bees and the mutually supportive activities of neighborhood, town and village life.

But this tradition is much broader than most people realize – well beyond farmers and food consumers, to include people with disabilities and local governments, neighborhood organizations and hardware store wholesalers, all together claiming a membership of 100 million Americans.

The stories in *Cooperation Works!* describe the breadth of cooperative action in the United States. Most importantly, the book charts future opportunities for building on these examples.

The diversity that is America is reflected by the diversity of cooperative examples presented in *Cooperation Works!*. This should not be surprising because cooperative organizations serve the economic and social needs of their members.

Words like "self-help" and "empowerment" have lost much of their meaning through overuse and misuse as platitudes rather than calls to action.

That's not the case in this book. Real stories of real people taking action, taking risks and getting things done remind us of what self-help and empowerment genuinely mean. The story of Ed Roberts and the other pioneers of the disability movement provide incredible examples of vision and perseverance.

Our society faces enormous economic uncertainties and challenges as we approach the turn of the century. This book reminds us that previous generations and many in our current generation also faced daunting problems – and found cooperative solutions to them. This should give us all hope that, just as in the past, working together collaboratively will help us solve the problems we are facing now and will face in the future.

The funding of this book was based on the same spirit of people and organizations working together as the cooperative stories the book describes. Four foundations and a university center, all with strong historical roots in the cooperative community, pooled their resources to make the writing of *Cooperation Works!* possible.

We hope that this successful example of collaborative funding by foundations will be replicated in the future. There are many wonderful stories to tell about the social and economic benefits of cooperative action and many media through which to tell them – books, radio, television, videos, the internet, cd roms, etc.

Cooperatively-oriented foundations, university programs and other organizations can play a critical role in getting this story out. And they can do it cooperatively.

William Nelson, President,
The Cooperative Foundation
& Cooperative Education Specialist, Cenex Foundation

Judy Ziewacz
Executive Director,
Cooperative Development Foundation

INTRODUCTION

If you are concerned that our society is becoming increasingly depersonalized or that it's getting harder and harder to get "good things" done, then this book will lift your spirits. *Cooperation Works!* is filled with stories of how people all over the United States are improving their lives and their communities by joining together in cooperative action.

In recent decades, roughly since the end of World War II, Americans have ceased to be united by a common cause. We have lost some of the cooperative values that sustained us in the past. We have lost the ability to work together to tackle the most pressing problems of our times. This book reacquaints us with the powerful things that cooperative action can accomplish – and *is* accomplishing in the United States today.

Through more than 50 examples, *Cooperation Works!* shows what people have done cooperatively to take more control over their lives, and it provides ideas on how the reader can take similar action.

COOPERATION AND COOPERATIVES

A cooperative (or co-op) is a business owned and controlled by the people who use its services. All co-ops share four additional features:

• **Service at cost.** This means that co-ops are not designed to maximize profits, but rather to provide goods and services to members at a reasonable price.

• **Benefits proportional to use.** Unlike for-profit businesses, co-ops distribute profits to member-owners on the basis of the *amount of business transacted* with the co-op during the year rather than on the *amount of capital invested* in the co-op. Credit unions and some co-ops plow profits back into the business each year to reduce costs or improve services instead of distributing them to members.

• **Democratic control.** In most cooperatives and credit unions, each member has one vote in decision-making regardless of the number of shares owned or the amount of business done with the co-op. Members elect the board of directors and vote on other issues at annual meetings or at other meetings held during the course of the year.

• **Limited return on equity.** The significance of this cooperative principle is that people buy equity in co-ops not to make a lot of money on their investments, but rather to enable the co-op to provide the products or services they want. They may get a return on their investment (usually 8 percent or less), but these dividends are a secondary issue.

Co-ops are different from for-profit businesses, which are owned by one or more investors whose intent is to make a profit by selling goods and services to other businesses and individuals. Co-ops are also distinct from non-profit organizations, which aim to provide educational, charitable and other services and which must reinvest any profits they make in their own operations or donate them to other non-profits or to government agencies.

Cooperatives can be divided into four main categories. **Producer cooperatives** are formed by farmers, craftspeople and other producers to purchase supplies or services and to market products. People form **consumer cooperatives** to buy groceries, financial services (e.g. credit unions) and other goods and services. **Employee-owned cooperatives** are owned by the people who work for the co-ops. For example, many cab companies in the United States are employee-owned. **Business cooperatives** are owned by for-profit businesses, cooperatives or non-profit organizations. Examples include wholesalers owned by retail hardware stores or fast-food franchisees.

Some businesses operate in a similar manner to cooperatives but are incorporated as for-profit businesses or non-profits. For example, many businesses have employee stock ownership plans (ESOPs), in which workers own a piece of the business. Many non-profit child care centers are controlled by parents and community representatives and operate in a "cooperative" manner.

The stories in this book are about cooperative action occurring in a wide variety of settings. Some involve formally organized cooperatives. Others don't. All describe people working together in a democratic manner toward a shared goal – and being successful at it.

COOPERATION, COMMUNITY, COMPETITION AND CONFLICT

The words cooperation and community connote teamwork or partnership. Conflict and competition indicate an adversarial relationship. *The authors believe that we would be healthier and happier as individuals and would function more effectively as a society if we treated one another primarily as partners rather than as adversaries.* We are still a long way from a society in which cooperation is the dominant ethic. But, as *Cooperation Works!* illustrates, there are many exciting examples in the United States today of cooperative action chipping away at old antagonisms and apathy.

There's no guarantee we will opt for new and better ways to work together in our communities, workplaces, schools and other institutions as we approach the 21st century. We could escalate current trends toward more conflictual relationships, such as the increasing violence and fear in some communities. Or we could withdraw into greater isolationism – in front of our television sets and computer screens – abdicating our roles as citizens and neighbors.

But, as this book suggests, we could make another choice and become better cooperators and community members. One of the reasons we think this a possible, and even likely, direction is that working together taps a deep human longing. Most of us have been fortunate enough at one time or another to be a member of a work group, a sports team, a community or church project, an educational experience, an extended family event or a similar effort in which the participants worked effectively together to get the job done. We know the special feelings of camaraderie and satisfaction that have come from these group efforts. Why can't we work to increase the likelihood that these experiences occur more frequently in our personal lives and in our society?

There's another reason why we believe that cooperative action has excellent potential to be the dominant way in which we relate to one another in the 21st century. *It works!* Judge for yourself whether the examples described on the following pages make a convincing case and whether there are ways in which the ideas and information presented can be of use to you.

PART I:
COOPERATIVE APPROACHES
TO BUSINESS

CHAPTER 1.

VALUE-ADDED AGRICULTURAL COOPERATIVES:
REVITALIZING THE FAMILY FARM

Since the last half of the 19th century, cooperatives have been a means for farmers to get a better deal in the marketplace. By purchasing supplies, borrowing money and selling farm products through co-ops, producers have been able to create a more equitable relationship with large agricultural companies and banks. But despite the bargaining power of agricultural cooperatives, family farms are on the endangered list in the United States – and so are the small communities that depend on them.

The value-added cooperatives that have emerged in North Dakota and Minnesota in the past two decades provide renewed hope for family farms, for agricultural towns and villages, and for all of us who value self-reliance and a sense of community. This chapter provides some background information on trends in American agriculture and some examples of how the value-added co-op model works.

ONE MAN LOOKS AT THE "NEW PHASE" OF AGRICULTURE

Dennis Gibson is a soft-spoken, thoughtful man. People listen to what he has to say. Gibson and his wife farm 1,800 acres in western Minnesota with his son, his sister and her husband. He grows sugar beets, corn and soybeans and also raises some deer in converted cattle pens.

Gibson joined the Southern Minnesota Beet Sugar Cooperative when it was first formed in 1975. "I guess I joined because I was young and a risk-taker," he says, "and because I trusted my neighbors who were organizing the co-op." His neighbors already had been growing sugar beets profitably for a number of years and had decided that a farmer-owned sugar processing plant would provide area farmers with an even better return than just growing the beets as a commodity.

The sugar beet co-op is just one of four value-added cooperatives of which Gibson is member. He also belongs to Minnesota Valley Alfalfa

Producers and Minnesota Corn Processors and is a founder of Prairieland Producers, a deer processing and marketing cooperative.

Gibson says he "kind of backed into the venison business." He got out of cattle feeding in 1981. In 1988, he decided he didn't want his cattle pens sitting idle anymore, so he began to raise deer. Soon he realized it would be more effective for a group of farmers to process and market deer meat together than for each producer to try to do it on his own. With some help from the Agricultural Utilization Research Institute (AURI) – a Minnesota non-profit organization that helps farmers and agricultural processors improve their access to markets and new technologies – Gibson and nine other deer farmers incorporated Prairieland Producers in 1992. The co-op is still in an experimental phase. It contracts with a private processor and deliberately has restricted its membership and production. As a result, the co-op has no debt and is gradually growing to meet new market demand.

Gibson had been interested in joining Minnesota Corn Producers (MCP) for a long time because, he says, "the co-op wasn't just producing ethanol but a wide variety of corn products, including fructose and starch." The co-op was originally formed in 1980 and began producing corn syrup, corn starch and byproducts at its $40 million plant in Marshall, MN, in 1983. It didn't become profitable until a few years later, but has prospered since then, building a $70 million plant in Columbus, NE, in 1992. Gibson purchased stock in the co-op in early 1995 when MCP offered an additional $150 million in stock to corn producers in Minnesota, Iowa, South Dakota and Nebraska in order to finance expansions at the cooperative's two plants.

"I got involved in the Minnesota Valley Alfalfa Producers Cooperative (MNVAP) for a different reason from the other co-ops," Gibson reflects. He's on the board of CURE (Cleaning Up our River Environment), which has as its primary goal to improve the water quality of the Minnesota River, the most polluted riverway in Minnesota. According to Gibson, "There are two ways to get farmers to change the way they farm: moral persuasion and economic incentives. I think the second way is much more likely to succeed. Alfalfa is a crop that's good for the soil and good for waterways. If the alfalfa co-op can find a way for farmers to make some money on their alfalfa, this will have a tremendous impact on the environment."

In the mid-1990s, MNVAP is collaborating with Northern States Power (Minnesota's largest utility), the University of Minnesota, Westinghouse, the United States Department of Energy and others to determine whether it makes sense to establish a large-scale alfalfa processing facility and an electricity generating plant fueled by alfalfa stems in western Minnesota. A key part of this analysis is to test the market for a wide array of alfalfa products ranging from different kinds of animal feeds to human food ingredients, pharmaceuticals and cosmetics.

If the business planning process identifies a profitable way to process and market the various alfalfa products, the co-op is projected to have an estimated 2,000 members and 180,000 acres of alfalfa in production by 1999. The biomass power plant fueled by alfalfa stems would generate 75 megawatts of electricity – enough power to meet the energy needs of a community of 45,000 people.

Gibson has been involved in the new value-added cooperatives for 20 years. His commitment is based on several factors: These co-ops make good economic sense for farmers; farmers reduce risks when they "diversify beyond corn and beans"; and the new co-ops help farmers become better stewards of the land.

"These cooperatives are just beginning a new phase in the evolution of agriculture," Gibson concludes. "There are going to be mistakes. Some co-ops will fail. Some people will try to take advantage of the current co-op mania. But I'm confident that there are many good co-op business opportunities out there that will succeed."

GETTING BEYOND THE COST-PRICE SQUEEZE

With a few minor deviations along the way, the history of U.S. agriculture in the 20th century has been one of rising costs of agricultural production and decreasing prices for agricultural products. The shorthand for this trend is "the cost-price squeeze." What it means is that for the past 90 years or more, family farmers have been getting squeezed out of farming. No matter how hard they have run to keep up, they have been gradually losing ground – literally.

In 1910, 15 cents of every dollar generated in the agricultural system went to the suppliers of agricultural inputs – seed, equipment, fertilizer and chemical companies, and lenders. The farm share was 41 cents; the remaining 44 cents went to marketing – transportation, processing, distribution, wholesale and retail businesses. By 1990, the farmers' share had plummeted to 9 cents, agricultural suppliers received 24 cents and the marketing share rose to 67 cents. In other words, the farmers' share of agricultural return in 1990 was less than one quarter of what it had been in 1910.

Family farmers have attempted to stay competitive in the marketplace by increasing their productivity; by introducing bigger and better farm equipment; by using more expensive and more effective chemical fertilizers and pesticides; and by attempting to increase the size of their farms. This strategy hasn't worked for most family farms. Since the end of the World War II, the number of farms in the United States has dropped from roughly 6 million to about 2 million. The average size of these farms has increased from about 190 to 480 acres. Both in 1980 and in 1992, approximately half the farms in the United States had gross sales of less than $10,000. The big difference is that the cost of living went up by 40 percent over those 12 years. In other words, the real income of these smaller farms dropped dramatically during this time.

The loss of two-thirds of the nation's farms in the past 50 years has been a problem not only for the farm families who have been displaced. It's also been devastating for many of the communities where they lived. In most rural communities, farms are the pump that primes the local economy. Farm loss has meant rural retail and service businesses going under, rising unemployment rates, outmigration, and the less quantifiable but equally destructive erosion of a community's social fabric and spirit.

There are urban consequences as well. As Sir James Goldsmith, a member of the European Parliament, states so clearly in his book, **The Trap**: "When people leave the land, they gravitate to the cities in search of work. But throughout the world there are not enough urban jobs and the infrastructure ... is already insufficient ... These are the indirect costs of intensive agriculture and they must be taken into account."

Why has this happened? The simple answer is that most farmers have been in a weak competitive position in the marketplace. They have had little or no economic clout in controlling the costs of inputs nor the value of outputs. Antitrust legislation in the late 1800s and early 1900s alleviated some of the most extreme distortions in the economic positions of farmers and agribusinesses. This legislation limited the ability of large companies to monopolize markets. It also prohibited the formation of cartels that had allowed groups of companies to collude on prices. Both of these practices put farmers at a terrible disadvantage in buying supplies or in selling farm products.

The growth of supply, marketing and agricultural finance cooperatives in the 1930s through the mid-1990s also has mitigated some of the worst aspects of farmers' vulnerability in the marketplace. In 1994, 2,200 marketing co-ops sold 31 percent of all U.S. farm commodities. In the same year, 1,600 supply co-ops sold 29 percent of the nation's farm supplies. The 240 farm credit cooperative banks and associations loaned 25 percent of all the money in U.S. agriculture in 1993. These co-ops provide a strong marketplace presence for American farmers.

Despite this presence, however, continuing trends throughout the 20th century clearly indicate that the cost-price squeeze persists. Some new mechanism to provide farmers with a greater role in the marketing of their farm commodities is needed if the family farm is to be more than a passing phase in American history.

VALUE-ADDED AGRICULTURAL COOPERATIVES

The value-added agricultural cooperative movement demonstrates that there is a way for producers to ease the pressure of the cost-price squeeze without leaving the farm. As the name indicates, the goal of these cooperatives is to add value to the raw materials produced on the farm and to return that added value to producers rather than to turn it over to "middlemen" – brokers, buyers, processors and distributors.

Value-added cooperatives are not a new phenomenon in the United States. Dairy cooperatives – including "Fortune 500" co-ops such as Associated Milk Producers, Land O'Lakes and Mid-America Dairymen – have been producing value-added dairy products on behalf of their farmer members for decades. Sunkist Growers, the large California-based cooperative that markets and processes citrus fruits, was started in 1895. Ocean Spray, with grower members in Massachusetts, Wisconsin, New Jersey, Florida, Oregon and Canada has long been a successful, creative processor and marketer of cranberry and other fruit products.

What is new is the unprecedented number of value-added co-ops that have formed or are in the process of being formed during the past few years. Most of these new co-ops are in North Dakota and Minnesota, two of the states hit hardest by farm losses in the 1980s.

Rather than acquiescing to the decline in the number of farms in the post-war period, some producers are investing in the long-term future of their farms and communities. Their strategy for making their farms profitable is to own post-production processing and marketing cooperatives. This strategy is not without risk. If farmers pool their funds and build a state-of-the-art pasta plant, as in one of the examples given below, the plant may or may not be profitable. Thus, producers can share in losses as well as profits. More and more farmers in the Upper Midwest are willing to take that chance.

So far, this "quiet revolution" on the Plains has been dramatically successful. None of the approximately 50 value-added co-ops financed by the St. Paul Bank for Cooperatives since 1973 has gone out of business. These new co-ops are owned by about 10,000 farm families; represent close to $2 billion in new rural investments; have created in the range of 5,000 direct new jobs and many times that number of indirect jobs; and have had a strong positive economic impact on dozens of rural communities and at least a minor positive impact on hundreds of others.

Besides "value-added," the second most applicable adjective for these co-ops is "diverse." In addition to the co-ops mentioned above and others to be discussed in more detail below, there are a bison cooperative; a number of corn processing co-ops that produce ethanol (a clean-burning alcohol used to boost the octane level of gasoline) and several others that make fructose (the primary sweetener in soft drinks and many other products); potato, pea, sweet corn and carrot co-ops; a hybrid poplar co-op that plans to market this fast-growing tree to the paper and pulp industry; soybean and pinto bean co-ops; pork, lamb and beef co-ops; an ostrich co-op, an emu co-op (a flightless bird imported from South America) and a tilapia co-op (a type of fish that grows well in aquaculture), all three in the development stage; and dozens more in operation or on the drawing boards.

It's too early to reach any grand conclusions about this quiet revolution. But its potential implications are enormous. These value-added co-ops may be showing the way to end or dramatically slow down the century-long death march of the family farm in the United States. Their economic and social impacts are substantial in the Upper Midwest, even though most are less than five years old. If producers in other parts of the country become cooperative entrepreneurs and increase the profits they receive from their farm products through this value-added model, this would signal a national shift away from what had, until recently, appeared to be an inevitable tightening of the vice on the family farm.

The next part of this chapter provides four examples of value-added cooperatives: the Southern Minnesota Beet Sugar Cooperative, the Dakota Growers Pasta Company, Organic Valley and Prairie Organic Cooperative.

SOUTHERN MINNESOTA BEET SUGAR COOPERATIVE

The Southern Minnesota Beet Sugar Cooperative was incorporated in 1975. It's one of four pioneering value-added co-ops formed during the 1970s and early '80s in Minnesota and North Dakota. American Crystal Sugar and Minn-Dak Farmers Cooperative – both sugar beet co-ops – were formed in 1972. Minnesota Corn Processors started in 1980.

During the first few years, Southern Minnesota Beet Sugar Cooperative didn't do nearly as well as its organizers had projected. Because of heavy losses and ineffective management, the banks foreclosed on the co-op's loan in 1978. Faced with two unfavorable choices – selling off the assets or selling the plant back to the farmers at a greatly reduced price – the banks chose the latter option. The co-op was thus able to get a second start with a much smaller debt burden because the value of its assets had been written down from $63 million to $19 million. The co-op has been profitable ever since.

When Dennis Gibson joined the co-op in 1975, he paid $200 an acre to purchase stock in the co-op. This stock purchase did three things: It provided capital for the co-op to begin operations; it committed Gibson to growing sugar beets for the co-op on the acres for which he purchased stock; and it committed the co-op to purchasing an agreed-upon acreage of sugar beets from him.

Thus, core financing and agreements on supply and demand were all taken care of in one simple membership contract. Each share Gibson purchased for $200 in 1975 is worth about $2,500 today. This means that another farmer interested in producing beets for the cooperative is willing to buy a share from Gibson – and thus the right to sell an acre of beets to the co-op – for 12.5 times the price Gibson paid. There are three main reasons why these shares have increased so much in value.

First, Southern Minnesota Sugar, American Crystal and Minn-Dak, all located in the Red River Valley, which forms the Minnesota-North Dakota border, have done a very effective job in cooperatively marketing sugar and byproducts from the sugar beet industry. Second, the United States government has had restrictions on sugar imports dating back to the early 1930s, including a sugar import quota that has been in effect since 1982. This quota has contributed to prices for domestically grown sugar that are well above the world price. And third, the three sugar beet cooperatives have maintained limits on membership and production, which have helped prevent a glut of domestic sugar in the marketplace.

THE DAKOTA GROWERS PASTA COMPANY

The Dakota Growers Pasta Company is owned by about 1,000 wheat farmers from North Dakota, western Minnesota and eastern Montana. The co-op built a state-of-the-art, $40 million pasta factory outside of Carrington, ND (population 2,700). The plant began operation in November 1993. Farmer-members provide all of the wheat processed at the plant.

In 1995, Dakota Growers produced about 100 million pounds of pasta in 50 different varieties for the private label, food service and ingredient markets. The plant employs 230 people. After only its second year of operation, the co-op generated $.46 per share profit, distributing $.31 in cash to farmer shareholders and retaining the remainder for operating reserves. What this means is that members not only received the current market price for the durum wheat they sold to the co-op, but they also earned a 20 percent annual return on their investment in the co-op. It's this combination of production earnings and sharing in the profits of milling and pasta processing that makes this value-added co-op a good investment for its farmer-members.

In early 1996, Dakota Growers issued new equity stock in order to finance a $5 million expansion to double the milling capacity of the plant. Confidence by wheat farmers in the co-op was so high that sales of stock far exceeded the stock sales target. The cooperative will use the additional capital as a reserve for future expansion of pasta production.

This farmer-owned enterprise represents a down-to-earth variation on "Field of Dreams." Farmers appeared to be building a factory in the middle of nowhere. In reality, they built it in the middle of durum wheat country – the wheat used to make spaghetti, ravioli, lasagna and other pasta noodles. The co-op allowed the members to shift from being commodity grain producers to processors of their raw products – and to reap the financial benefits from this expanded role.

There are community and population impacts as well. North Dakota lost 10 percent of its rural population between 1980 and 1990. Employment at the pasta plant in Carrington alone equals about 9 percent of the city's population, and this doesn't take into account the on-farm, construction, transportation, service and retail jobs created directly and indirectly by the plant.

ORGANIC DAIRY AND GRAIN PRODUCTS

Organic farming has a special niche within value-added agriculture. "Organic" means that agricultural products are grown without the use of synthetic fertilizers, herbicides and pesticides, and, in the case of animals, without antibiotics or hormones. Most states have regulations defining what is and what is not organic. There are also private agencies which certify that farms and processors meet organic standards. In 1996 or 1997, the small variations in state and private criteria for organic will be replaced by a uniform set of national organic standards administered by the United States Department of Agriculture.

Up until the end of World War II, the vast majority of farmers in the United States farmed organically. They just didn't call it that. Over the last 50 years, however, about 99 percent of U.S. farmland has become chemically dependent. In the past decade or so, farmers have begun to explore ways to reduce their use of chemicals for a variety of different reasons: environmental or health concerns, reduction of input costs, market opportunities, and stricter state and federal environmental regulations.

Organic farming is part of a broader movement called sustainable agriculture, which means using farming techniques that can be carried out for the indefinite future without degrading the land and water. Sustainable agricultural practices generally involve one or more of the following: reduced chemical use (sometimes called integrated pest management), increased use of plant and animal manures, reduced tillage, and rotational grazing of livestock. All these practices have in common a reduction in purchased inputs: petroleum products, other chemicals and machinery.

Sustainable agriculture in general and organic farming in particular have the potential to challenge the "cost-price squeeze" discussed above on the input side as well as the output side. For example, an organic farmer may reduce his or her cost of farming by substituting green manure and animal manure produced on the farm for chemical fertilizer. Crop rotation and nonchemical weed and insect management can replace herbicides and pesticides. Rotational grazing of animals reduces the amount of feed and the cost of hay harvesting and storage. At the same time, animals fertilize the fields while they graze, thus reducing manure handling and application costs. Organic farming is generally more labor-intensive and may have lower yields than conventional farming. Thus, increased labor and lower volume of production need to be balanced off against reduced input costs.

In general, however, organic farming helps producers beat the cost-price squeeze in two ways: They can spend less on the things they need to run their farms; and they can get a premium price because some consumers are willing to pay more for organic vegetables, fruits, dairy and grain products, and meats for reasons of health, nutrition and the environment. On top of these economic incentives to producers, the added benefit is an environmental one: Organic farmers are stewards of sustainable farmsteads.

Some of the organically grown grains and beans produced in the United States are exported to Western Europe and Japan. However, most organic foods are consumed domestically. Even though organic foods are less than one percent of all food consumed in the United States, their consumption has been rising by 20 percent per year or more during the past few years. Organic food cooperatives are playing a big role in this rapid increase. Because of the way they are grown, organic products have "added value" before they even leave the farm. To the extent that producers join together to process and market their products, they can add value to value.

Coulee Region Organic Produce Pool (CROPP) is a dairy, egg and vegetable cooperative headquartered in southwestern Wisconsin. Dairy products account for about 90 percent of the co-op's sales. As of early 1996, CROPP had about 80 family farm members in Wisconsin, Iowa and Minnesota producing about 3.5 million pounds of milk per month. CROPP has had some growing pains since its start-up nine years ago, but during the past few years the co-op has been profitable, while at the same time paying a premium price to its members about 25 percent above the going rate for raw milk. The co-op produces a wide array of organic dairy products: milk, 20 kinds of cheese, yogurt, ice cream, spreads and butter – at 11 small dairy plants scattered around the Upper Midwest and at two plants in California. Most of CROPP's dairy products are marketed nationally and under its own brand name, "Organic Valley."

CROPP's current plan is to double its production during the next four years. The increasing consumer demand for organic products and the soon-to-be-announced national organic standards will make organic dairy products and other organic foods a rapidly growing industry well into the 21st century.

Prairie Organic Cooperative completed its first full year of operation in the spring of 1996. At that time, the co-op had 50 members with about 20,000 acres of organic grains that were committed to be marketed through the co-op. Prairie Organic is headquartered in Bismarck, ND, near the center of the state. In addition to North Dakota, the co-op's membership is from Montana, South Dakota and Minnesota.

In 1995 and early 1996, the co-op sold a little more than $1 million worth of organic grain – 60 percent from members and 40 percent from nonmembers. The co-op's goal is to double its membership and acreage in 1996 so that it will cover all its operating expenses through its grain sales. A second goal is to expand into organic meat processing and marketing. Prairie Organic is negotiating with North American Bison Cooperative to have organic beef processed at the bison co-op's plant in North Dakota.

The two biggest obstacles in the marketing of organic grains have been inconsistent supply and unreliable quality. Food companies and retailers will not make major commitments to organic cereals, bread products, pastas and other grain-based products unless the supply and quality can be guaranteed. They don't want to go through the expensive process of testing, promoting, packaging and securing shelf space for new product lines and then run out of stock or receive quality complaints from consumers.

Solving supply and quality problems is exactly where Prairie Organic comes into the picture. The co-op is developing close working relationships with key organic grain buyers and works out agreements with them on types and quantities of grains to be grown by co-op members. The co-op also negotiates prices and quality requirements. Eventually the co-op wants to develop a reserve system in which grain will be set aside from year to year in order to address shortages that may result from bad weather or higher-than-expected demand.

As a farmer-owned co-op, Prairie Organic is in a unique position to solve these marketplace problems. The co-op can coordinate the kinds and amounts of grain production of its members. It can establish quality standards and provide training and inspection services to make sure the standards are met. The co-op also can address a unique logistical problem of organic grains. They cannot be commingled with conventional grains because they would lose their organic premium. The separate storage, transportation and processing of organic grains is necessary to avoid infestation by pests or contamination by synthetic chemicals. Thus, for the most part, organic grains are stored on the producer's farm until they are ready for shipment to the processor. Coordinating grain inventories on dozens of farms and arranging for just-in-time delivery from these diverse storage points requires a complex computer system not unlike that used by long-distance delivery services. Prairie Organic is in the process of developing such a system.

CONCLUSION

In the past two decades, and particularly in the first half of the 1990s, value-added agricultural cooperatives have provided a glimmer of hope after decades of family farm decline and depopulation of rural communities. Through these co-ops, producers have shifted from defense to offense. Instead of being dependent on marketing agents and processors, they have become their own "middlemen," taking on additional risks, but also sharing in the increased value of their products.

Rising costs of agricultural production and declining or stagnant prices for farm commodities have been more than offset for these co-op members because they are no longer selling commodities, but rather processed products with higher profit margins. Organic co-op members and other sustainable farmers are reducing their costs of production, as well, by replacing purchased inputs with on-farm resources.

Does this mean that the cost-price squeeze that has put 4 million family farms out of business in the past 50 years is a thing of the past? Not at all. It does mean, however, that the value-added cooperative model may provide a strategy for family farms to become more profitable and, thus, for their operators to have a greater incentive to stay in farming. It also may provide a means for the revitalization of thousands of rural communities that benefit from increased producer income and from locally owned marketing and processing facilities.

The use of this strategy is increasing rapidly in the Upper Midwest. But is it a passing fad that will fade away quickly, especially if there is a big failure or two? Can it work in other parts of the country? How can information on the do's and don'ts of this model be transferred from one part of the country to another? From one group of producers to another?

There are no easy answers to these questions. There are, however, a couple of underlying points about the value-added agricultural co-op model that should be stressed. First of all, they have worked well so far. The older value-added co-ops – such as Land O'Lakes, Sunkist and Ocean Spray – and the sugar beet co-ops are proof of their ability to endure and prosper. Second, the economic premises on which they are organized are sound. They have reduced farmers' dependency on "middlemen." In addition, tying equity investments by producers to an internal system that controls supply and demand of products within the co-op has worked well to maintain the cooperatives' profitability over the long term.

Thus, the strategy is a proven one. Whether it will continue to be applied effectively in the Upper Midwest and to spread to other parts of the country remains to be seen. But there is no question that these value-added cooperatives have the potential to bring about a profound shift in American agriculture and to reinvigorate thousands of agriculturally based rural communities. It's up to family farmers themselves and to those who work with them as cooperative, agricultural and rural advocates and developers to realize this potential.

ACKNOWLEDGMENTS

Harriet Behar, Organic Valley Cooperative, Viroqua, WI
Frank Blackburn, Minnesota Assoc. of Cooperatives, St. Paul, MN
Lee Estenson, St. Paul Bank for Cooperatives, St. Paul, MN
Allen Gerber, Minnesota Assoc. of Cooperatives, St. Paul, MN
Dennis Gibson, Farmer, Montevideo, MN
Chris Hanson, Univ. of Minnesota Center for Alternative Plant and Animal Products, St. Paul, MN
Dennis Johnson, St. Paul Bank for Cooperatives, St. Paul, MN
Jim Kusler, Prairie Organic Cooperative, Bismarck, ND
Jack Paela, North Dakota Cooperative Coordinating Council, Mandan, ND
Bill Patrie, North Dakota Rural Electric Cooperative Assoc., Mandan, ND
Liz Reinhiller, North Dakota Growers Pasta Company, Carrington, ND
Sue Retka Schill, Northern Plains Sustainable Agriculture Society, Langdon, ND
Will Schill, Prairie Organic Cooperative, Langdon, ND
George Siemon, Organic Valley Cooperative, Viroqua, WI
Ann Woods, Midwest Organic Alliance, St. Louis Park, MN

REFERENCES

Bird, George. 1988. "Sustainable Agriculture : Current State and Future Trajectory." East Lansing, MI: Michigan State Univ. Dept. of Entomology.

Egerstrom, Lee. 1994. **Make No Small Plans: A Cooperative Revival for Rural America.** Rochester, MN: Lone Oak Press. (Good source of information on the origins and current examples of value-added co-ops.)

Goldsmith, James. 1994. **The Trap**. New York: Carroll and Graf.

Kraenzle, Charles A. 1996. "Cooperatives' Share of Farm Marketings Hits 14-Year High." *Rural Cooperatives*. January-February: 4-5.

Minnesota Assoc. of Cooperatives. 1994. "The New Generation of Cooperatives: The Next Chapter in Community Development," Year in Cooperation. St. Paul, MN: Minnesota Assoc. of Cooperatives. Fall. (Year in Cooperation does an excellent job of providing updates on value-added agricultural co-ops as well as on other innovative co-ops in the Upper Midwest.)

Minnesota Assoc. of Cooperatives. 1995. "Commitment to Community," Year in Cooperation. St. Paul, MN: Minnesota Assoc. of Cooperatives. Fall.

Fortunato, Henry and David J. Thompson. **A Day in the Life of Cooperative America**. 1994.Washington, D.C.: National Cooperative Bank.

CHAPTER 2.

THE COOPERATIVES BEHIND THE SMALL BUSINESSES ON MAIN STREET

Walk down Main Street America and you'll see business cooperatives at work. For instance, your local newspaper gets fast-breaking news from the Associated Press. Your favorite supermarket may well get supplies, advertising support and other services from a wholesaler co-op. Your neighborhood pharmacy might belong to a purchasing co-op, which helps your local pharmacist compete in a marketplace that's become increasingly discount-store dominated.

These are but a few examples of business cooperatives that today move billions of dollars' worth of goods and services nationwide. Indeed, business co-ops are the backbone of support for many of this country's small businesses and their owners. This chapter takes an in-depth look at one family's experience as part of a hardware cooperative. It also describes co-ops in numerous other industries, especially the fast growing cooperatives serving many fast food franchisees.

THE ANDERSON FAMILY'S STORY

On any given day you'll find Jennifer Anderson, president of Davis Lumber and Hardware in Davis, CA, walking through her store, answering customers' questions as she goes. She's a trailblazer in a normally male-oriented business. Whether it's an inquiry about choosing a front door, or selecting the right type of outdoor light or finding the necessary part for a plumbing repair, Anderson knows the answer and where the item can be found in her store.

That's no small feat, considering that Davis Lumber and Hardware is housed in four buildings, stretching for two city blocks that run alongside the railroad tracks laid when Anderson's grandfather started the business in the early 1900s. The store has departments not only in hardware and lumber, but also electrical, plumbing, pet supplies, housewares, furniture, a nursery center, mill shop, a rock yard and a custom frame shop. Employing 100 people, Davis Lumber and Hardware is Davis' largest downtown business. Due to its size, longevity and use by thousands of loyal customers, it's not just a hardware store, it's a community institution.

Anderson's grandfather, A. Gordon Anderson, emigrated from Canada to the Davis area at the turn of the century. In 1914 he opened the hardware and general store, which also doubled as a bank of sorts for the community's cash-starved farmers and ranchers. Later, Gordon served as the city's mayor for 13 years. When he died in 1937, the family exchanged the store's inventory for stock in the Auburn Lumber Company, a chain of local lumber yards. Then in the early 1950s, the Auburn Lumber Company hired Gordon's son (and Jennifer's father), Donald Anderson, as manager for the Davis store. By 1962, Don Anderson had bought the business back into the family's hands.

Today you get a sense of this history as you climb the stairs to the company's main office, passing photos of the original store and turn-of-the-century Davis. Like many hardware stores throughout the country, Davis Lumber and Hardware is a time-honored family and community tradition. Looking at those photos, Anderson says, "I'm reminded that we wouldn't be regarded as we are now if each generation of the Anderson family hadn't committed themselves to being the best business of our kind in town."

Yet, like most family-run hardware stores today, their market share is under attack from the discount stores and national chains, which now account for more than 30 percent of the annual $120 billion sales of the hardware industry. The family-based owners can't rest on their laurels, as the next "big box" store could be just around the corner.

Jennifer Anderson is well aware of that. Her entrance into the hardware industry goes back to age 10, when she was ceremoniously placed "in charge" of dusting at her family's store. Soon her job expanded to include pricing and then cashiering. She loved working in the business, which she did through high school, saving her money to buy her first car.

Later, however, Anderson couldn't wait to get away from Davis. Smitten by the ideals of the 1960s, she traveled around the West Coast, attended three different universities looking for herself and studied all the in-vogue humanies courses. Then one day in a retailing class at the University of Montana, she found herself saying, "This is where I belong." Soon after, she enrolled at Wilkes University in Pennsylvania and earned a degree in marketing.

When it came time to do career planning, Anderson approached her father about working again for the family business. He advised her to get a job somewhere else first and test her wings. She landed a job at a major Sacramento department store, where she honed her retail skills. Then in 1980 her father was diagnosed with cancer, and a year later he asked her to join the business – with the idea that she'd take it over. By 1985, she was the company's president.

Anderson belongs to a new breed of hardware retailer. She knows the competition she's up against, and she's geared to continually improving and developing the business. The Sacramento regional market is hotly competitive, with many retail choices for the do-it-yourself consumer. Recognizing the limitations of a one-store operation, Davis Lumber and Hardware had joined Ace, one of the nation's leading hardware wholesalers back in March 1966, making it one of the first Ace stores on the West Coast.

Back then, of course, Anderson was still in college and was little aware of the benefits of Davis Lumber and Hardware's relationship with Ace. To her, Ace was just a supplier, like any other, except that her family had a sizable investment in the organization. But as Anderson's involvement in the family business grew, so did her appreciation of what Ace did for its customers. Ace itself shifted its focus in 1976, from being a privately owned wholesaler to being a retailer-owned support organization.

THE ANDERSON/ACE PARTNERSHIP

Now Anderson uses her own retailing skills in partnership with an energized Ace organization. And she sees the results coming through loud and clear. Today her store is in the top 100 of Ace's 5,000 member stores. In June 1994, Anderson was elected to the 11-member Ace board of directors, becoming the first woman board member in Ace's history. She also chairs the company's Retail Success Committee and is a member of the Audit, International and MIS (Management Information Systems) Committees.

Clearly, Anderson is highly active in the Ace organization today. She cites the following key roles that Ace fulfills for its members:
• providing services beyond just product and buying power to help members become better retailers,
• assessing the right product for the right customer,
• providing multiple deliveries,
• providing leadership in the industry, making it the best of the hardware co-ops,
• keeping up with changes in the industry,
• supporting store planning, electronic ordering and leading-edge technology, and
• providing strong identification with the Ace name, through a national program focused on neighborhood stores.

An important element for the locally owned hardware dealers is how to differentiate oneself in a competitive market. "Not everyone wants to go to a 'big box' store," Anderson explains. Ace helps its members to create a distinct retail image, setting them apart from their competition, through a program called the Competitive Partnership Alliance. While participation is voluntary, Ace is striving for high member involvement. Because Ace focuses its efforts on member service, it has become the most efficient national wholesaler by industry standards. In 1996, Ace is working hard to pass True Value (another member co-op) as the nation's number one hardware wholesaler. In 1995, True Value did an annual volume of $2.437 million, and Ace had $2.436 in sales.

Anderson says she sees both strengths and weaknesses in the Ace relationship. On the one hand, Ace buys to meet local needs through its 14 strategically located distribution centers. The organization never tells members what to buy, what to stock or how to run their businesses. On the other hand, customers view Ace almost like a franchise, thus expecting to get the same things at every Ace store in the country. But, in fact, Ace members are so diverse in what they offer in the markets they serve and in their size that they can't be uniform in product or offer the same store layout. Nor would they want to. Customers' needs are different throughout the country. This presents a challenge for Ace as it grows: How does it to present itself nationally to its millions of customers?

When Davis Lumber and Hardware first joined Ace, all its transactions were with the office and warehouses in Chicago. As Ace grew, it set up a regional system of support and delivery. The first regional warehouse was in Benicia, CA, which moved to Rocklin, near Sacramento, in 1988. Ace's Rocklin Distribution Center serves approximately 55 member stores in the Sacramento metropolitan region and 310 others in northern California and Nevada. Of these stores, owners of 30 of them meet quarterly to discuss problem solving, mystery shopping, and training and education. Each region has a retail consultant, whose job is to help the local members. The consultant works with store owners and suggests ways to improve standards and operations.

There are also 150 Ace advertising groups throughout the country that meet regularly to discuss their needs, advertising programs and advertising placement. This is the most active of the member dealer groups affiliated with Ace.

Today, the owner dealers have a shared vision of what they want to be and what they want Ace to be. They have a lot of confidence in the future because they believe they are meeting a community need. As Anderson notes, "There's plenty of business for the Ace dealers as long as we're committed to running a successful business. Ace has the capacity to help us to grow and achieve our goals."

ACE LOOKS TO THE FUTURE

Ace was first formed by a small group of Chicago-area retailers in the early 1920s. Although privately owned, the organization utilized a number of cooperative practices to develop customer loyalty. Incorporated as Ace Stores, Inc., in 1928, the company named Richard Hesse as its first president, a position he held for 44 years.

Hesse introduced semiannual dealer conventions to bring Ace dealers together in one common marketplace, at one specified time, to see the products and promotions available to them. To this day, conventions remain a key activity Ace offers to its dealer-owners. Emphasizing its low-cost program and expanding its merchandise offerings, Ace grew dramatically, reaching sales of $25 million by 1958. By the time Ace became a fully dealer-owned cooperative in 1976, annual sales had soared to $382 million.

Since 1978, Ace has averaged about one new retail-support center per year. These centers are strategically located in 15 regions across the United States. Each center stocks some 60,000 items – carrying both national and Ace brands – giving the Ace dealer the type of inventory and local delivery service so vital to the dealer's business progress.

A strong Ace identity program, which included a new logo, was initiated in 1987. As part of that, Ace's national television, radio and print campaigns, along with Ace-identified stores and spokesperson John Madden, work together toward increasing the individual Ace dealer's sales. The Ace image is to support the concept of the neighborhood hardware store with the "helpful hardware man (or woman)." Other dealer services – including data processing systems and "store of the future" planning – serve to spell out more sales success for all Ace dealers.

Ace's policy of high-profit retailing and low-cost distribution continues to be the solid foundation upon which the company consistently grows and prospers. These policies and Ace's commitment to being a retail-support company to its dealers continue to attract the more progressive hardware stores and lumber dealers. Today Ace's dealers number 5,000 nationwide, with accounts in more than 55 countries and territories. But for Ace and its dealer-owners, such as Jennifer Anderson, this is just the beginning.

Today a program called Ace 2000 aims to enable Ace dealers to become the best retailers in their respective markets by the year 2000. "The New Age of Ace," announced in October 1994, is an acceleration of the Ace 2000 process. Its strategy utilizes advanced technology, improved store design, and top-of-the-line managerial and retail programs. The target objective is to grow Ace to $5 billion in wholesale sales by the end of this century.

FROM HARDWARE TO HOTELS

Besides Ace, there are other hardware buying co-ops that serve the vast majority of the more than 22,000 independent hardware stores in the United States. True Value, ServiStar and Coast-to-Coast are but a few of these cooperatives. By pooling their annual sales of more than $10 billion, smaller hardware stores can use their buying power to attack the price advantage of the big chains and maintain a competitive edge. The training sessions and national conventions run by the wholesale co-ops strengthen the professional capacity of the member stores and their staffs. True-Value and Ace, in particular, run extensive national advertising campaigns that associate consumers with their local hardware store. Many of the hardware co-ops are now more proactive in helping their members develop their retail business to gain market share. To build volume in a highly competitive market, many of the co-ops have crossed borders to branch out into Canada and Mexico to develop retail partners.

Hardware co-ops are just one of many types of business cooperatives that are helping small businesses remain competitive in today's complex marketplace. Let's look at a few other industries in which co-ops play a key part.

NEWS SERVICE

The oldest business cooperative in the United States is the Associated Press, which was launched in 1848 by six newspaper owners in New York City. Independently, each had been spending more and more each year to obtain news from around the world. By starting a cooperative and sharing the cost, they were able to obtain equal access to news. Thus, Associated Press sparked a revolution in both news gathering and business cooperation. Today, nearly 150 years later, Associated Press is the world's largest news-gathering service. From its headquarters in the Rockefeller Center in New York City, it sends news to the pages of its 15,000 member newspapers around the world.

GROCERS

In the grocery industry, almost 20,000 supermarkets, food stores and convenience stores are members of regionally based wholesale cooperatives. There are 31 regional co-ops in the United States doing more than $50 billion in sales per year. One of these is New Jersey-based Wakefern, which is one of the largest co-ops by volume in this country. Having nearly $4 billion in annual sales, it serves its member Shoprite stores mainly in the mid-Atlantic states. Wakefern and the other wholesale cooperatives provide their members such services as advertising, inventory, insurance, and financing for equipment and expansion. The National Cooperative Bank works alongside many of the retailer owned cooperatives to provide a range of financing tools to meet the needs of the independent retailers.

Besides regional food wholesale co-ops, there are also national cooperatives. One of these is the nearly 50-year-old Shurfine, a private-label marketing and procurement co-op that supplies 33 wholesale warehouses, which in turn supply 12,000 retailers. Shurfine sales topped $1 billion in 1995, and it increased its market share to 9 percent. A similar national wholesaler is Topco, a buying co-op for 40-plus supermarket chains. Among the other buying co-ops are some that serve specialty markets for ethnic foods or convenience stores.

SHIPPING

More than 100 shipping cooperatives deliver goods to their thousands of small- and mid-sized shipping company members. These cooperatives consolidate both truck and rail freight deliveries and obtain volume discounts. They began this activity more than 100 years ago when the completion of the Trans-Continental Railroad made national distribution possible. Some shipping cooperatives have a general membership, some are regional and some are specialized, such as those serving department stores, furniture stores, confectionery manufacturers and book publishers.

PHARMACIES

The Independent Pharmacists' Cooperative based in Madison, WI, supplies its more than 1,800 member pharmacies in 20 states. The co-op contracts with the wholesaler for a cost-plus-percentage price, with all discounts passed on to the co-op members. The co-op brokers over $500 million annually and handles $60 million in volume directly. The co-op began in 1984 and now has 25 staff. There are other regional pharmacy co-ops, such as Legend in the East and Leader in northern California. Leader's ranks swelled to 42 members over the past few years and is now doing joint purchasing of more than $50 million for its members. In an industry that has had no new pharmacies open up in the past few years and with many having closed, cooperative purchasing is the only tool for survival. Community-based pharmacies are using their purchasing co-ops to battle the giant discount stores and to win HMO contracts, which generally exclude independent pharmacies.

CARPETING

Yet another business cooperative example is Carpet Co-op of America, commonly known as Carpet One. Since its founding in 1984 by 10 carpet retailers in an Atlanta hotel room, the co-op has grown to a staff of 100, with some 450 members serving 700-plus stores. Recently, the co-op opened its membership to retailers in Australia, Canada and New Zealand. The retail volume of its members in 1995 was $2.6 billion, and the co-op paid $15 million in dividends to its members last year. The founders felt that the lack of dealer organization put local retailers at a disadvantage against their competition. Carpet One arranges volume purchasing by the members who end up buying from 50 percent to 95 percent of their carpets from the co-op. Carpet One now owns worldwide rights to the Bigelow line, the oldest mill in the United States. Carpet One also has two wholly owned subsidiaries, which are both co-ops. Other member services include national advertising materials, research, improved merchandising and sales training.

HOSPITALITY

Best Western began as a cooperative association in 1946 and is now the world's largest lodging brand. Its members operate more than 3,500 independently owned and operated hotels, motor inns and resorts, providing 283,374 guest rooms. The cooperative started out by providing a mutual referral business for its members. Today, Best Western International operates in 62 countries. The annual dues are applied to marketing and operational support services. Best Western's worldwide, toll-free reservation system handles more than 60,000 calls daily during the peak season and books approximately $725 million annually in room sales. In 1995, almost 52 million guests stayed at Best Western's member hotels and spent more than $7 billion at these hotels.

These business cooperatives are only a sampling of the co-ops playing a key role in building American business. There are hundreds more. Doctors, dentists, bakers, stationers and gasoline dealers are just some of the groups practicing the art of cooperation in business. The examples here point out the tangible benefits already obtained by visionary business leaders who saw where their industries could go. These leaders understood that they could only grow and improve through vertical integration to achieve economies of scale. Through their cooperatives, members can control their own specialized organization, compete effectively with the chains and work with their fellow members to enhance their professional capabilities.

FRANCHISEE COOPERATIVES

Recently, franchisees discovered what independent businesses have practiced successfully since 1848: the small business cooperative. The first franchisee co-op was formed in 1955 when Dairy Queen Pacific NW, the regional distributor, was bought out by the local franchisees.

However, the real breakthrough for the concept of a business cooperative for fast-food franchisees began with Dunkin' Donuts. In 1974, it began a pilot project to test the idea of a franchisee-owned and controlled purchasing cooperative. The pilot program was a success, and by 1976 all five Dunkin' Donut regions had their own purchasing cooperatives. These co-ops protect their member store owners against product shortage, utilize volume leverage, consolidate distribution efforts and establish prices in advance so that store owners know what they'll have to pay in the future. About 95 percent of the more than 1,400 Dunkin' Donut shops are franchises, and almost all participate in the purchasing co-ops. When you're selling nearly 4 million donuts and more than 1 million cups of coffee a day, volume co-op purchasing greatly increases net margins.

Another franchisee co-op leader is the Food Service Cooperative, which began as the Kentucky Fried Chicken Purchasing Cooperative in 1978. The KFC cooperative emerged due to difficulties franchisees were having with their purchasing arrangements. Fortunately, one of the franchisees was James Cornett, a leader with more than 20 years of management experience in farm supply cooperatives. It was agreed to hire a management consulting firm to study the total system and determine how to supply the retail units at the lowest cost. The upshot was that a co-op was deemed the best option. The Food Service Cooperative now provides services to Taco Bell and Dairy Queen franchisees. Totally separate from the parent franchisers, the co-op supplies both company and franchised units. The co-op, which had revenues of $4.5 million in 1979, closed out 1994 with annual sales of $528 million. By 1995, the co-op was owned by more than 500 franchisees from all 50 states.

Threats, not just opportunities, can give birth to co-ops. Such was the case with the creation of Arcop, Inc., a co-op Arby's helped create as a way to protect the company during its chapter 11 proceedings in the 1970s. The concerned franchisees joined together to use the co-op to maintain control over their supplies. The co-op acts as the broker of purchases without taking title to supplies. The individual franchises pay the suppliers, yet benefit from the volume discounts negotiated by Arcop. Arcop uses only one distributor and has no role in shipping and warehousing.

In California, one franchise model went even further. When the Straw Hat Cooperative Corporation incorporated in 1987, it joined a long list of respected American companies that operate the cooperative way. What was unique about Straw Hat was that they were the first franchisees to also own the franchiser. The co-op originated out of the sale of the Saga Corporation to the Marriot Corporation. Not wanting the Straw Hat Pizza franchise component, Marriot arranged to sell Straw Hat to Pizza Hut. Most of the franchisees notified Pizza Hut they would not convert, and they then negotiated the creation of an independent co-op. The approximately 100 Straw Hat franchisees in California and Arizona take a great deal of pride in owning their franchise.

The recent spate of mega-mergers, acquisitions and leveraged buyouts is having an effect on the franchise world. Some franchise systems saddled with debt and a downturned market face a questionable future. Control over the future becomes a critical factor for franchisees whose life savings are at stake. In almost all cases, franchisees have a strong desire to form purchasing co-ops and replace Wall Street ownership with Main Street ownership.

CONCLUSION

Business cooperatives serving independent businesses and franchisees are making a difference in the way this country does business. Their dynamism and entrepreneurial leadership on behalf of their thousands of members add a vibrant element to our complex economic system.

For small-business owners, cooperative membership offers distinct advantages, such as purchasing power, advertising clout, keeping up-to-date in the industry, sales training, new technology – to name a few. The National Cooperative Bank sees this as a tremendous niche for its services to cooperatives. As a result, the Bank has put together a number of financial services and loan products that can help the small business and franchise co-ops be financially strong in this competitive marketplace. Having a bank that understands their business provides these co-ops with an understanding financial partner. Business cooperatives also face challenges, a key one being: How do you keep the "hometown store" feel in a national-scale enterprise?.

Still, there's no question that without their cooperatives, thousands of small businesses would fade into extinction, unable to stand up against the national chains. Business cooperatives enable small businesses to thrive and be competitive in the marketplace. What's more, these co-ops are helping to preserve the special small-business qualities that make Main Street America a favorite place to shop.

ACKNOWLEDGMENTS

Jennifer Anderson, President, Davis Lumber, Inc., Board Member of Ace, Davis, CA

Stanley Dreyer, Vice President, National Cooperative Bank, Washington D.C.

Paul Hazen, Senior Vice President, National Cooperative Business Assoc., Washington D.C.

REFERENCES AND SOURCES

Ace Hardware Corporation. 1995. *Ace Continues to Plan for the Future.*.

Fortunato, Henry and Thompson, David J. 1994. **A Day in the Life of Cooperative America**. Washington, D.C.: National Cooperative Bank.

National Cooperative Bank. 1995. "National Cooperative Bank 100."

Turner, Melanie. 1994. "Ladder of Success." *Davis Enterprise*. Dec. 4.

CHAPTER 3.

CONSUMER CO-OPS:
AROUND THE CORNER & ACROSS THE COUNTRY

City dwellers and farmers alike can drive to a co-op in Scottsbluff, NE, to do their weekly food shopping, buy a new car muffler or get their car washed. Government employees in Los Angeles shop at any of 11 outlets of a membership department store to buy everything from food to furniture. And people living across the country can buy tents and hiking boots at any of the 50 retail stores nationwide of a Seattle-based co-op.

These are but a few examples of the hundreds of consumer cooperatives scattered across the United States. Diverse in products and location, these co-ops all offer their members quality products at a reasonable price – a mission that can be traced to the earliest consumer co-ops begun in this country more than a century ago.

This chapter will study four highly successful consumer cooperatives that sprang from different roots in different decades.

FROM "OLD WAVE" TO "NEW WAVE"

Consumer cooperatives can trace their origins in the United States to the mid-1800s. At that time, labor union members, immigrant groups and various reform organizations launched co-ops to bring the prices of consumer goods within the reach of financially struggling workers and to create an alternative to the company store.

This trend continued into the next century. The Great Depression saw the launching of thousands of consumer co-ops, as federal and state governments assisted co-ops as a means of alleviating hunger and poverty. Many of these co-ops, often called the "Old Wave," vanished with the advent of post-war prosperity. Fewer than 100 survive to the present day, most of them in the rural Midwest.

But it was in the 1960s and '70s that consumer co-ops took another leap, with the forming of food co-ops in many communities. This "New Wave" of cooperatives emerged in the era of movements: civil rights, anti-war, back-to-the-land, the first Earth Day of 1970. The food co-ops saw themselves as an alternative economy, with a focus on community control and concern for the environment. Created in the spirit of the 1960s, these co-ops have emerged to become the entrepreneurs of the 1990s.

FROM "HIPPIE STORE" TO FORMIDABLE ENTERPRISE

In the small university town of Davis, CA, the Davis Food Co-op (DFC) occupies the second largest retail site downtown and is the second largest local employer. With 1995-96 sales of $8 million, the co-op is Davis' largest locally owned retail enterprise. The co-op's 4,500 active member households purchase 12 percent of all food retail sales in this city of 50,000 people. With an expansion of its retail space to be completed in 1997, the co-op will be a $10 million business before the end of the century. By then, DFC will be among the top 10 food co-ops in the United States by volume and the largest single co-op food store by square footage.

The story of how a small natural foods buying club rose to become such an important local business is one of vision, innovation, adaptability to change, strategic choice, leadership and luck. Begun in 1972, under the leadership of Ann Evans, DFC operated as a buying club for many years. To increase service and selection, members later decided to rent a 400-square-foot garage where they could store more items and open up a retail operation for a few hours each week. Membership grew, and in 1978 the co-op moved into a space about three times larger. With this new location's "real store" look, even having windows, it seemed like paradise to members. Many of them worked hard to convert the space into a natural foods store.

The phrase, "build it and they will come," applied to the new location. The co-op flourished and reached several milestones: hiring a permanent staff and manager, electing a board of directors and incorporating. The more the co-op offered, the more it attracted members. The co-op was certainly a "very '70s" event. Only members could shop there, and each household had to contribute two hours per week working at the store. Food issues brought out tremendous passions and sometimes division among members. It was a time of lively discussion about the co-op's future direction. One group wanted it to become more oriented toward the entire community, while another wanted to maintain the "small is beautiful" philosophy. The arguments on both sides were compelling and showed the depth of thinking about the nature of American business. Like other food co-ops, DFC has had to grapple with the question: How can co-ops maintain their philosophy in the midst of the explosive growth of the natural foods industry?

The dialogue in Davis was challenged by an event that set the co-op on its unique path. In 1981, Safeway, a supermarket chain, vacated its 22,000-square-foot downtown location, leaving many downtown residents feeling abandoned. Only one other small neighborhood market remained in the area. Meanwhile, the co-op's growth pressured members to think about their next move. Eventually, DFC asked members to consider relocating into one-half of the old Safeway space, by this time owned by a different landlord. Members voted against the plan (55 percent con versus 45 percent pro) in November 1981; the size was too daunting, the economics too scary. Another supermarket took the location; however it operated marginally for a couple of years and then closed.

In the meantime, the co-op was bursting at its seams and needed another site. The DFC board negotiated a more attractive lease and sale of equipment, which it felt comfortable in presenting to the membership. This time members overwhelmingly approved (76 percent), and a new era began for DFC.

The co-op's move to downtown Davis in 1984 was marked by lots of hope and limited capital. At first, the co-op didn't attract the expected volume and began to run at a loss. To make matters worse, the landlord unexpectedly gave the lease back to Safeway, which gave DFC an ultimatum: either rent the entire 22,000 square feet or vacate the premises. With nowhere else to go, DFC reluctantly signed a lease for the entire building and took on an additional $5,000 a month in lease payments. Fortunately, the Davis Free Clinic was looking for a larger location. It leased 5,000 square feet from the co-op in 1986, and DFC turned its energies to figuring out how to succeed at the downtown location.

Motivated by the fear of going out of business, the co-op agreed to radically alter its way of doing business. It charged newly hired general manager, Dennis MacLearn, with the task of turning DFC around. MacLearn and the board made several key changes over a two-year period, such as changing the work requirement to voluntary and altering the share capital requirement to raise more money. Results were slow in coming, but after six months sales began to climb. The slump was over, and the co-op was on its way.

For the next two years DFC saw double-digit sales increases every month. The co-op had become a true supermarket and an increasingly important downtown retail location. Part of the turnaround was due to winning two city block grants in 1986 and 1987 totaling $45,000, which was used to remodel a 3,400-square-foot portion of the building. A cafe, a bookstore and a pizza takeout moved in, making the co-op's building now fully rented. By 1988, sales hit $2.9 million. Soon after, the other downtown food market closed, and DFC became not just the natural foods supermarket in town, but also the *only* supermarket downtown.

Just a few years after sitting down with Safeway and pleading for its retail life, the co-op once again asked to meet with Safeway. Safeway's property manager was incredulous; the small, once-almost-bankrupt co-op was now offering to buy the building. On December 27, 1990, with a $1 million loan package from the National Cooperative Bank and National Cooperative Bank Development Corporation and an infusion of share capital from a member fund-raising drive, the co-op became owner of the site. For the members this was one of the proudest moments in the co-op's history. Today DFC is the only supermarket in Davis that owns its own site.

Within about a year of each other, the cafe went out of business, the bookstore owner decided to go to Europe, and the pizza operator relocated to Oakland. The co-op saw an opportunity to expand into the center of the building. Remodeling was completed in 1991 with an additional loan from the National Cooperative Bank Development Corporation and a vote by the members to increase their annual share investment from $15 to $20. This gave the bank the comfort that cash from both earnings and share investment would strengthen the co-op and put the co-op into a better position to repay the loans.

The new high ceilings, spacious layout and attractive colors transformed the store, and sales took another leap. Under the guidance of general manager Karl Krueger, who came on board in 1991, the co-op's image has continued to shift from that of "hippie store" to being recognized as a formidable retail enterprise in the city.

But there's another side to DFC's image that is just as important. As the people in Davis know, DFC is living proof that, unlike the chains who come and go, co-ops are committed to their communities.

Many co-ops in other communities are taking the same types of actions as DFC to grow and meet consumer need. For example, Seattle-based Puget Consumers' Co-op (PCC) – with seven stores, nearly 45,000 members and annual sales of $43 million – is the largest consumer-owned food co-op today. The two largest single-store food co-ops in the United States – Hanover Consumers' Co-op in Hanover, NH, and the Hyde Park Cooperative Society in Chicago – date back to the Depression. They are thriving with annual sales of more than $20 million dollars each, and both will open second stores by 1997. Such moves certainly herald a new era of confidence in the cooperative way of doing business. Developers are now more eager to meet consumer and community needs by having co-ops in their shopping centers.

According to *Cooperative Grocer*, an industry trade magazine, 300 retail co-ops with 500,000 members and 3,000 buying clubs with

100,000 members now exist in the United States. The food co-ops' combined retail volume is more than $500 million.

For the scores of successes, however, there are failures. Hundreds of buying clubs started in the same era have closed down, many small co-op storefronts have failed, and some small co-ops now operate marginally. The food co-ops should be studied to determine what factors determine success or failure.

That query is not just an academic exercise; it's linked to future survival. What began as a counterculture movement is now an industry. Food co-ops were the first retailers to bring natural foods closer to the mainstream. But now these co-ops face stiff competition in the billion-dollar natural foods market sector. Natural foods chains created in the 1970s and '80s have become the dominant retailers. The largest of these is Austin, TX-based Whole Foods Market, which as of 1996 had more than 50 stores and $500 million in annual sales. It plans to have 100 stores by the year 2000. The Whole Foods format is a sort of "Walmart" of natural foods stores; their huge-store format and buying power dwarf the competition.

Only by taking advantage of their circumstances and upgrading their capacity can DFC and other natural foods co-ops remain successful. They need to find niches to withstand the competition. And they need to grow to a size that meets their customers' enhanced expectations about service and product. Growth of the existing co-ops is therefore a prerequisite in order to evolve from mere survival to success.

A CO-OP SERVING CITY AND COUNTRY

The Panhandle Cooperative Association in Scottsbluff, NE, began operations in 1942. Since then the co-op has made strategic, innovative decisions to link its farmer base with its consumer members in the twin cities of Scottsbluff-Gering, population 24,000. Today the co-op is one of the area's key enterprises and the largest local employer, with about 350 staff members. It has 15,000 active members and annual sales of more than $50 million from its varied operations.

The co-op is a part of the Farmland regional system of cooperatives, which comprises the largest co-op in America with almost $7.3 billion in 1995 sales. The Panhandle Co-op uses the Farmland logo on many of its buildings and on its farm-supply and petroleum products.

Panhandle is indeed a varied venture. In Scottsbluff and surrounding communities it operates a shopping center and supermarket, an appliance store, a grocery store, two convenience stores, four fertilizer plants, a feed store, a car care center (which includes a Midas Muffler franchise, a car wash and a tire shop) and several gas stations.

The co-op's structure separates its activities into agricultural and retail divisions. In terms of dollars, the agricultural division does two-thirds of the total volume. The mix of consumer and farmer operations has affected the co-op's primary banking relations. It means that certain agricultural activities are eligible to be financed by CoBank, whereas the more consumer-oriented operations can be financed by the National Cooperative Bank.

What makes Panhandle different from other farm supply co-ops is its strategic decision to become a consumer form of cooperative to meet the needs of both its urban and rural customers. Bob Pile, Panhandle's controller, believes the impetus for that decision goes back to 1948, when Farmland (then called the Consumers Cooperative Association, or CCA) decided to sell a supermarket it owned in Scottsbluff. The Panhandle Cooperative Association bought the business from CCA to begin serving consumers in the city as well as farmers in the countryside.

Then in 1975, the co-op closed the old supermarket and purchased a 40-acre site in Scottsbluff to build Panhandle Plaza. Plaza Foods, now Scottsbluff's largest supermarket by size at 44,000 square feet, also has a deli-bakery, a flower shop and a pharmacy. More than 14,000 member/customers shop at Plaza Foods each week. The rest of the Plaza, which has four major buildings in all, includes administrative offices, the largest feed and tackle store within a 150-mile radius, a gasoline station and the car care center.

Under a new manager, Don Wiseman (1987-91), the co-op took a different look at its operations. First, Panhandle did a major remodel of the shopping center and created a separate subsidiary corporation as a development arm. The Plaza had been developed in the boom era of the 1970s, but in the downturn of the 1980s, the Plaza's space was underutilized. Through the new corporation, the co-op invested in a Bonanza Steak House franchise to fill a space next to the supermarket.

Franchises often are made available to individual families or closely held business corporations. In this case the franchisee was the cooperative. Unfortunately, the Bonanza Steak House became unprofitable and was closed in 1995. The corporation created to develop opportunities did not achieve the expected results and is now a corporation on paper only. For Panhandle, creating a separate business corporation for development showed a potential that was never realized mainly due to the downturn in the economy at the time.

In November 1988, Panhandle invested in a Midas Muffler franchise to complement the services of the car care center. Virgil Hagel, who went to work for the co-op in May of that year, became supervisor of the project. Panhandle was only the second co-op in the country to obtain a

Midas franchise. With Hagel's experience in other co-ops and in the automotive industry, the franchise operation got off to a good start.

As general manager, Wiseman had a number of reasons for going after the franchise. He was concerned that the word "co-op" implied membership only, and he wanted to develop business opportunities to strengthen Panhandle Plaza's image. Bringing a nationally known name such as Midas into the center seemed like a good idea. It would draw the general public to Panhandle Plaza and show that it was oriented to all consumers, not just to farmers. Midas came to Scottsbluff, made a presentation to the co-op and the co-op became a franchisee.

Hagel believes the Midas relationship is valuable both for the co-op as an enterprise and for him professionally. In their local Midas ads, they run the co-op and Farmland logos alongside the Midas logo. They believe that the combination gives consumers a strong image of local ownership and regional strength combined with national capacity. Because of the unit's reputation, they are able to attract quality employees, which translates into low turnover in the Midas shop. That, Hagel knows, changes the way the co-op looks at customers and their vehicles. As for the co-op, it benefits from the Midas name recognition and excellent warranty program. The co-op is proud that in its eight years, only one complaint has been registered with the Midas Corporation. The net result is that the franchise keeps the cash registers ringing, and the unit adds a strong profit margin to the co-op's overall operating statement.

Wiseman continues to support the idea of co-ops investing in franchises. Now he's general manager at the Sun Ray Co-op in Texas, which owns a Hot Stuff Pizza franchise. He believes co-ops should consider franchise operations that meet members' needs. For him, the franchise is a proven way of doing business with a national track record. It takes the experimentation out of developing new operations from scratch and adds the national name recognition that draws local response. Once the franchise concept was explained, Wiseman felt it received strong board support. In fact, he feels the Panhandle board was progressive on the innovation. It was much more difficult, he notes, to get the franchisers to accept the co-op as a franchisee.

Today Plaza West contains the Midas shop, a tire shop, a bulk oil facility and a battery service center. To the east of Panhandle Plaza sit a gas station and self-service car wash. To top off the diversity found at the site, there's also a golf driving range and a putting green.

The people served by Panhandle's various enterprises are not all members. However, becoming a member is simple; there is no fee to join. At the end of each year, the co-op's board reviews financial results and declares a patronage dividend of generally from 1 percent to 2 percent. Co-op members get this dividend based upon the total dollar purchases they make from any of the co-op's operations. The co-op usually dedicates 30 percent to 40 percent of the patronage dividend as a cash payment to members and credits the remainder to the member's share account. The rest of the net savings is kept by the co-op.

The patronage dividends applied to stock continue to build until the member has $200 in stock; at that time he or she becomes a voting stockholder in the association. The dividend continues to be retained at the level set annually by the board until the member has $2,500 in co-op shares. At that point, 10 percent of the amount allocated to the member's shares above $2,500 is also paid back in cash. The entire program is computerized and the cash rebates are sent out about two weeks before Christmas. The success of the co-op in attracting customers to become members is evidenced by the fact that 72 percent of the sales are to members.

The board is governed by a 10-member board of directors who elect the chairman. The CEO of the association holds the title of president but is not a board member. Generally there are one or two members of the board who come from Scottsbluff, with the rest being farmers or coming from the rural areas. At this time there are 7,500 stockholders eligible to vote and generally a range of 2 percent to 4 percent of the members vote in the annual board election. The board has put increasing effort into getting members to the annual meeting. Last year they had 700 people attend. There was an excellent dinner, a humorist, reports from the co-op's chairman and president, plus a special report from the president of Farmland Industries.

Panhandle also invests time in member activities. They mail a quarterly newsletter to all members. The newsletter contains advertising about many of the co-op's products and services. The co-op also holds regular "Member Appreciation Days." At one such event recently, the co-op cooked hamburgers and garlic sausage at each branch. Many of the co-op's suppliers came to the locations to give presentations and samples. Concurrent with the event, the co-op provided advertised specials in all departments from grocery to petroleum.

Panhandle is one of a number of farm supply cooperatives that have shifted their missions to meet the needs of small, rural American towns. By meeting consumer need and filling a range of retail niches, Panhandle has remained healthy and change-oriented. Not everything has worked, to be sure, but the key has been the will to innovate. With that kind of spirit, farm co-ops have ample opportunity for continued success in rural America.

IN SEARCH OF A BETTER AX

One of the most successful cooperatives in the United States is Seattle-based Recreational Equipment, Inc., better known as simply REI, which saw total annual sales for 1995 of $435 million. REI operates nearly 50 stores nationwide and has a mail order catalog with a growing international base. It also owns a travel adventure company and two subsidiaries that manufacture tents, clothing and recreational equipment.

REI was founded in 1935 by a group of Seattle mountaineers. One of the founders went shopping for an ice ax and couldn't believe the $17.50 price tag he found at one outlet. Outraged at the prices and quality compared to what could be found in European shops, he and fellow climbers decided to band together in their buying efforts. Their first joint purchase was for ice axes from Austria, with a great price of just $3.50 each. Indeed, cooperation worked!

In the book, **REI: Fifty Years of Climbing Together**, Harvey Manning tells the story of this unique cooperative organization. For a time, Lloyd and Mary Anderson, two of the founders (also members no. 1 and 2) operated what grew to be a flourishing buying club out of their home. As the group looked at their future, they could see their venture outgrowing the Anderson's house. Some of the members encouraged the Andersons to go into business for themselves. However, the latter didn't want to profit from doing business with their friends.

The group sought an organizational form that reflected their democratic interests and related to the members. They also wanted an economic form that rewarded loyalty and shared the profits with users. They didn't have to look far. In the 1930s, Seattle was a hotbed of co-op activism, with many consumer co-ops, a large student housing co-op, some worker co-ops and much talk of utopian communities.

The original REI group decided the co-op form would best meet their needs. Mary and Lloyd Anderson visited the Washington Student Co-op to study its operation. They also met with Ed Rimbauer, a Seattle attorney and co-op supporter, who helped them form "The Recreational Equipment Cooperative" as an unincorporated association in 1938. Because of his commitment to the cooperative movement, Rimbauer did all the legal work for free.

The co-op's first retail location was a humble shelf at the Puget Sound Cooperative on Western Avenue near Seattle's Pike Place Market. The Puget Sound Co-op manager donated his services to help launch the new recreation co-op. By the end of 1938, REI had 82 members, $1,361 in gross sales and $212 in dividends paid to members. Little were the founders to know that the dividend program – a part of most co-ops at the time – would one day be a major feature setting REI apart from its competitors.

The next leap for the co-op was in 1948, when it issued its first catalog describing a 300-item inventory. This year also marked the 10th anniversary of the co-op, with membership at 2,700, annual sales at $28,000 and dividends at $2,000.

After operating the co-op for nearly 20 years as an unincorporated association, the co-op leaders were advised to incorporate. The state law for cooperatives required the issue of stock, which the co-op didn't have. As a result, the board chose to continue the co-op form of organization under the state of Washington's non-profit law. At the annual meeting in 1956, the co-op members voted reluctantly to accept Recreational Equipment, Inc. as the new name, as state law no longer allowed use of the word "co-op" in their legal name.

One of REI's proudest moments was in 1963, when sales manager and later CEO Jim Whittaker became the first American to ascend Mt. Everest. As equipment manager for the expedition, Whittaker assembled the 14 tons of gear needed by the 19 climbers and 37 Sherpas for the four-month expedition. The successful climb propelled Jim Whittaker into fame. His name was everywhere, as was REI's name on his equipment. The height of this success was an invitation to the White House from President John F. Kennedy. Many people even encouraged Whittaker to seek political office in the Pacific Northwest, where he was now a legendary figure. After Kennedy was assassinated, Whittaker accompanied Robert Kennedy in 1965 on the first ascent of the newly named Mt. Kennedy in Alaska.

By 1968, REI gained its 100,000th member, reached sales of $3.5 million and paid out $300,000 in dividends. The next decade would be one of substantial change. The first member, Lloyd Anderson, retired as manager at the end of 1970. Replacing him was Whittaker, whose commitment to growing REI was paramount in an age of post-war optimism – and markedly different from Anderson's Depression-era caution. Whittaker wanted to spread the co-op message and boost REI's prospects in a growing market that anticipated more competitors.

One of Whittaker's first moves was to open REI's second store after nearly 40 years of doing business. The city of Berkeley, CA, easily became the choice for the expansion experiment. There, in a city of co-op activism, REI already had 10,000 members buying from its catalog. A year later, REI opened another store in Portland, OR, and then a year later a fourth store in Carson, CA. Thus, the march of REI stores across America had begun, reaching nearly 50 stores by 1996.

Since the 1970s, REI has continued its managed growth pattern and presently opens three or four stores a year. As the nation's largest consumer cooperative, REI projects membership of more than 3 million by the turn of the century. It returns the majority of its earnings to members, with annual returned earnings having reached a level of more than $20 million by the mid-1990s.

As a result of its solid successes, REI contributed more than $600,000 in 1995 to protect the outdoors for recreation. Total conservation contributions over the past two decades equal more than $4 million. By 1996, REI had more than 4,500 employees and had twice been voted as one of "the 100 best companies to work for in America" in a book by that title. REI ranks number 73 on the National Cooperative Bank Co-op "100 list" for 1995.

FIFTY YEARS AND STILL GROWING

Any new resident of southern California asks a number of questions after living there a few months: Why do they call it Hollywood? What happens in downtown L.A.? What is FEDCO, and why are their parking lots so full?

FEDCO (Federal Employees Distributing Company) is a unique type of American retail operation. Its powerhouse presence in southern California is obvious in its numbers. Sales for 1995 were more than $700 million. Each of FEDCO's 11 stores draws 8,000 to 10,000 shoppers daily and is open seven days a week. Each year FEDCO welcomes some 20 million shoppers and has more than 5,500 employees working at all levels of retail, distribution, warehousing and administration.

FEDCO's beginnings date back to post-World War II. Concerned about post-war inflation, Congress had frozen the salaries of federal employees in 1948. How could working people keep up with the cost of living if they couldn't gain higher wages? The answer was to buy consumer goods at lower cost. A small group of federal post office employees in Los Angeles initiated the idea of buying at wholesale and selling at retail. The enthusiastic organizers were able to sell hundreds of lifetime memberships at just $2 each, and FEDCO was born as a member-owned non-profit organization.

By the following year, the first 800 members had chipped in $1,600, and FEDCO opened its first retail location. The original members fixed up a showroom on North Broadway in Los Angeles, ran the store as volunteers and started with one paid employee. Like the first co-op store in Rochdale, England, founded in 1844 FEDCO opened with just a few items on the shelves: radios, toasters, irons and the like. In FEDCO's case, those items were samples because the co-op didn't have enough money to buy inventory. So members came to the store, looked at the samples and paid for their choices in advance. This helped FEDCO's tenuous cash flow and allowed it to place volume orders directly with wholesalers.

The organization grew steadily by meeting the needs of an expanding federal workforce in Los Angeles. The population boom in southern California meant more families, more houses and more demand for consumer goods. FEDCO was in the right region at the right time.

However, the 1950s were also the era of strict fair trade laws, under which manufacturers set the retail price of an item and restricted distribution of their products to those retailers who maintained that price. That, of course, was counter to FEDCO's mission. On behalf of its consumer members, FEDCO either had to fight or die. It became one of the few retailers to take the price-fixing battle to court. Eventually FEDCO won, and the "fair trade" restrictions were defeated. FEDCO's members and all consumers benefited from the victory. Edward Butterworth, who led FEDCO's legal fight, is now the company's president.

The decade of the 1950s also marked another key change at FEDCO. Membership, which had originally been limited to federal government employees, was extended to include state, municipal and local government employees. Later, college students and people on Social Security were also added to the member eligibility list. The membership fee set at $2 in 1948 is still only $10 today. A venture that opened its doors in 1949 with 800 members now boasts more than 4 million members.

Today each FEDCO outlet is a full-line department store offering its members more than 150,000 units of quality merchandise at low prices. The administration and distribution center in nearby Santa Fe Springs ensures that everything runs smoothly every day. Each store houses 40 different merchandise departments that sell everything from furniture to food. In addition, there's a pharmacy, an optical department and discounted referral services (real estate, residential improvements, automobile and so on). The attractively displayed merchandise differs in every aspect from the warehouse-type store so common in today's retail environment. The FEDCO stores range in size from 140,000 to 240,000 square feet. All stores are free-standing and provide on average 1,200 parking spaces per site.

The opening of a new FEDCO store is a major event in southern California, guaranteed to draw a crowd of 30,000 people. FEDCO is North America's largest member-owned department store chain and is proud of its success. Continued strong, stable growth has been the hallmark of FEDCO's progress, with its commitment to the slogan: "Members are our first concern." In 1999, FEDCO will celebrate its 50th anniversary and its unique role in American retailing.

CONCLUSION

The stories of the consumer cooperatives in this chapter clearly illustrate the diversity among the co-ops sharing this category. They evolved for different reasons, in different ways, in extremely different marketplaces. Yet one common thread runs through all their histories: They all sprang into existence to meet their members' needs. Indeed, staying in tune to those needs – rapidly changing as they are – is the key to consumer co-ops' future prosperity.

No successful consumer co-op today can rest on simply "doing what we've always done, in the way we've always done it." As the examples in this chapter have shown, consumer co-ops need to constantly stay open to innovation. That may mean finding new ways to reach more people, such as Panhandle Cooperative's decision to serve both the rural and urban inhabitants in its area. It may mean exploring new approaches for keeping old members and capturing new ones, such as the challenge increasingly faced by natural foods co-ops as they watch nationwide chain competitors move into their communities and adopt their people-oriented practices.

Now more than ever, consumer co-ops need to build on their old strengths and pinpoint new ones. It's not an easy task. Consumer co-ops will continue to find ways to balance conflicting goals. How do they expand, and yet stay in touch with diverse memberships? How do the people running these co-ops become astute business professionals while maintaining the "not business as usual" philosophy that attracted members in the first place? How do they meet the spiraling fierce competition in the retail world and still keep their cooperative principles firmly in sight? Consumer co-ops will need to grapple with answers into the 1990's and beyond.

ACKNOWLEDGMENTS

Bridgette Boudreau, Member Relations Specialist, Puget Consumers Cooperative, Seattle, WA

David Gutknecht, Publisher, Cooperative Grocer, Athens, Ohio.

Virgil Hagel, Automotive Department Manager, Panhandle Cooperative Assoc., Scottsbluff, NE

Paul Hazen, Executive Vice President, National Cooperative Business Assoc., Washington, D.C.

Ginni Hines, Corporate Secretary, Panhandle Cooperative Assoc., Scottsbluff, NE

Karl Krueger, General Manager, Davis Food Co-op, Davis, CA

Bob Pile, Controller, Panhandle Cooperative Assoc., Scottsbluff, NE

Kathleen Robins, Assistant Marketing Director, Davis Food Co-op, Davis, CA

Theresa Steig, Member Relations/Marketing Co-ordinator, Puget Consumers Cooperative, Seattle, WA

Doug Walter, Membership Director, Davis Food Co-op, Davis, CA

REFERENCES AND SOURCES

Laning, Chris. 1993. **Looking Back: A Davis Food Co-op History (1972-1984)**. Davis, CA: Davis Food Co-op.

Manning, Harvey. 1988. **Fifty Years of Climbing Together**. Seattle, WA: Recreational Equipment, Inc.

Thompson, David J. 1994. "The FEDCO Phenomena: Member-owned Retailer is a Major Player." *Cooperative Business Journal*. April: 5.

Thompson, David J. 1994. **Weavers of Dreams: History of the Founding of the Modern Cooperative Movement.** Davis, CA: Center for Cooperatives, Univ. of California.

Thompson, David J. 1989. "Davis Food Co-op: Turnaround Tale." *Cooperative Grocer*. April/June: 13-16.

CHAPTER 4.

ENTERPRISING BUSINESSES OWNED BY THEIR EMPLOYEES

Plywood mill workers in the Pacific Northwest, nurses in Minneapolis and cab drivers in the nation's capitol may not seem to have much in common. But some among these diverse groups are linked by a key factor in their day-to-day lives: They own the companies they work for, through worker cooperatives.

According to the Directory of Workers' Enterprises in North America., last published in 1991, there were then about 150 worker cooperatives in the United States, employing 6,500 member-owners. At that time, slightly more than half of those co-ops were found in four states: California, Washington, Massachusetts and Minnesota.

As workers strive to gain more control over their working environments and their job security, cooperative ownership of companies is becoming an increasingly attractive option. This chapter will look at the origins and operations of three worker co-ops that have emerged as models and industry leaders.

APPEAL ACROSS THE SPECTRUM

Many of today's worker co-ops grew out of the counterculture of the 1960s and '70s. The people who launched these organizations had two main objectives in mind: They wanted their companies to meet a social or community need, and they wanted their workplace to be run on a human scale, with democratic control and management.

While many of these early organizers were white, educated and middle-class, the people involved in starting worker co-ops have since become more diverse. Members of many of today's worker co-ops are working-class or belong to ethnic minorities. Churches and community organizations within the black and Hispanic communities also have given birth to many worker co-ops. Also, as minority-based economic development corporations have gained successes in new business startups, a logical next step has been to spin off those enterprises and let the employees buy them.

In the current era of budget cuts, voices of such people as long-time self-help guru Robert Woodson have been joined by more conservative advocates, such as Jack Kemp, 1996 vice presidential candidate and the former secretary of the Department of Housing and Urban Development during the Bush administration. Increasingly, worker co-ops are seen as self-help enterprises that can break old cycles of dependency on government assistance. While welfare and other help dwindle, problems don't simply vanish for those trying to climb out of desperate situations. Worker co-ops present another route that holds promise.

Another twist on worker ownership of businesses is the Employee Stock Ownership Plan, or ESOP. The Boston-based ICA (Industrial Cooperative Assoc.) Group, a main force behind development of worker cooperatives, also is pioneering in the area of ESOPs, which combine tax benefits with a mechanism for democratic control in the workplace. Currently, there are some 11,000 ESOPs in the United States, employing more than 11 million workers, with total corporate equity amounting to more than $70 billion.

While only 2 percent of companies in the United States have ESOPs, these have racked up some impressive results. For instance, the most recent version of **The 100 Best Companies to Work for in America** by Milton Moskowitz and Robert Levering shows that of those top 100 businesses, 30 have ESOPs. The ESOP structure offers much potential for growth of employee-owned companies in the United States.

Whatever form the structure may take, worker-owned companies have carved out a prominent place in today's business scene. The remainder of this chapter will look at a few pacesetters.

HOPE AND HOME CARE

A business is growing in the South Bronx. And lots of people are taking notice. This poor, economically neglected neighborhood is the birthplace of Cooperative Home Care Associates (CHCA), a company employing 300 home-care workers, mostly African-American and Latino women, many of them single mothers. CHCA has become a model for similar enterprises in other cities across the United States. The company also gained recognition as one of three "Entrepreneurs of the Year" cited by *Inc.* magazine in 1992.

CHCA's beginnings can be traced back to 1985, when Rick Surpin was working for the Community Service Society of New York. His research showed that home health care was an industry with a 20 percent growth rate. He noted that Medicare cutbacks meant that hospitals were sending people home early to reduce costs of care. The number of people needing home health care was rising rapidly, and with a larger percentage of the population becoming elderly, future decades would see an even greater demand.

Surpin also observed that home-care agencies operated like temporary personnel agencies, with part-time contract employees, low wages and high employee turnover. He saw a tremendous opportunity to turn poor-quality jobs into better-paid positions through a worker cooperative. Surpin then raised foundation money to subsidize the creation of CHCA and became its first executive director.

CHCA began with 12 aides and had revenues of $220,000 in 1985, its first year. A decade later, CHCA's revenues had soared to more than $7 million. It has evolved from a subsidized experiment to a totally independent firm owned and controlled by its worker-members.

The key to CHCA's success is its structure as a worker cooperative. After a three- month trial period, a CHCA worker becomes an owner-member by committing to build a $1,000 equity investment through a weekly payroll deduction of $3.50. When equity reaches $50, the member gains voting rights in the co-op. Members elect six of the nine-member board of directors and guide the enterprise by serving on committees. The board of directors meets once a month and has responsibility for overall operations. There are four member assemblies per year that set polices and cover training issues.

Members share in CHCA's profits, which amount to about $300 per member per year, or a 30 percent return on their investment. Workers receive health benefits, sick leave, paid vacation and training. The average hourly wage is $7.25, which is 16 percent above the home-care industry average. When wages are added to other benefits, the total package makes CHCA's workers the best paid in the industry.

Perhaps the most astounding part of CHCA's success story is that 85 percent of its workers were once on welfare. It generally takes a CHCA worker from six to nine months to get off welfare. At $7.25 an hour, with a 32- to 34-hour workweek, it's a challenge for many to make the leap from welfare to work. Yet they do it!

CHCA's format pays off for everyone. Turnover is only 20 percent, compared to a 40 percent turnover rate in most major home-care firms, according to the Visiting Nurse Service of New York. CHCA members believe that giving the worker-members a stake and a say in the company provides both financial incentives and a sense of involvement.

Take, for example, the story of Florinda DeLeon, a divorced mother of three and an immigrant from the Dominican Republic. She was once unemployed and doing volunteer work in the Bronx. When a friend noticed that DeLeon helped the elderly members of her parish get dressed to go to church, she suggested that DeLeon get a job in the field. Soon DeLeon went to work for CHCA as a home health aide. Now she's also an assistant instructor and has served as an elected board member.

During her term on the board, she told a *New York Daily News* reporter that because she and her fellow workers set the policies and salaries, "we decide what's best for us." Those few words sum up CHCA's benefits to its members as they move from welfare to financial self-reliance.

One reason why home care is a complex industry is that clients require only a few hours of care at a time – some irregularly, others regularly. Thus, home-care workers travel from home to home and work in isolation. To overcome these challenges, CHCA developed an atmosphere of mutual respect and support for co-workers. For example, CHCA guarantees its workers a minimum 30-hour week. This provides economic security and produces higher morale in a traditionally low-pay industry.

CHCA accepts only one of every four job applicants. Selection is based on maturity, patience, hard work and reliability. About 80 percent make it through the first three months of training and move on to employment; only about 80 percent of those survive the crucial first six months. Much of the training is dual-language to meet the needs of the large Spanish-speaking workforce and CHCA's Spanish-speaking clientele. The Home Care Associates Training Institute has grown to include 15 full- and part-time staff.

The educational level of most new workers at CHCA is low, so training posed a challenge. Most workers had hated school, so why would they love classroom lectures now? CHCA recognized the problem and developed its own method of hands-on demonstrations accompanied by peer teaching. Having workers actively participate ensures that training remains lively and engaging.

Indeed, training is the foundation of CHCA's high-quality performance and its ability to stand up to stiff competition to get contracts from social service agencies and Visiting Nurses Associations, the sources of most of CHCA's business. By providing quality care at a competitive cost, CHCA is a major player in the contract health-care industry. Many of its major contractors see CHCA as their best quality provider. CHCA's standards of reliability and competence and its low incidence of patient complaint add up to a model image for the industry.

Currently, the Ford Foundation and the Charles Stewart Mott Foundation are sponsoring the establishment of home-care models in four other cities. The first of these was Home Care Associates in Philadelphia. HCA began in February 1993 with 12 employees and a first-year revenue of $200,000, which climbed to more than $1 million in 1994. HCA now has 70 workers and is described by the Visiting Nurse Association as being the largest home-care provider in Philadelphia – and their highest quality provider. HCA became profitable six months ahead of schedule.

Another company modeled after CHCA is Cooperative Home Care in Boston, which opened in March 1994. With 35 aides, CHC already has reached the break-even point financially.

The possibilities for the CHCA model seem endless. The United Hospital Fund of New York reports that in 1994, 7 million people received some form of health care in their homes. Medicare and Medicaid now spend $18 billion annually on home health-care services. These numbers of people in need and dollars spent are expected to grow for many years. Such a need requires a massive response.

The value of CHCA lies in its having linked an underserved market (home health-care consumers) and a group needing better working conditions (home health-care workers). Thus, CHCA is indeed a grass-roots solution that makes both economic sense and good social policy. In a world in which so much of our society's foundation appears to be crashing down, CHCA's model is busily lifting people up.

REVOLUTIONARY BREAD

Michael Gierkout strides through the busy bakery, weaving between the bread trolleys and the many production lines. Here and there he stops to explain the process to the visiting delegation of Japanese government officials. After a half-hour of peering into vats, watching the machines manipulating dough and inspecting the many ovens, you begin to see why Alvarado Street Bakery is the largest organic bread baker in the United States. The bakery makes bread, bagels and tortillas using sprouted wheat instead of flour. They take whole, organic wheat berries and soak them in filtered water for about three days until they sprout. The living sprouts are then ground into dough to make a flourless, nutritious bread.

Listening to Gierkout talk, you hear the pride in his voice. He explains the thoroughness and constant experimentation that goes into everything they do. The commitment at Alvarado Street is to making the best quality product they know how. As a pioneer in a growing industry, the bakery must earn its leadership role. It has no interest in matching the mass production of Wonder Bread. You can tell by the many workers here that the Alvarado Street Bakery has merged the virtues of modern machinery with the care and commitment of the old-fashioned baker. Not only that, the aroma that rushes out of the bakery into the surrounding streets should be bottled and sold.

But the group of Japanese visitors is not here to study organic bread baking. They're here to learn about Alvarado Street Bakery's structure of worker ownership. The bakery is a thriving business and a worker cooperative. It began as a non-profit in the heady days of 1978. Initially called Food for People, it was part of a loose-knit group of activists committed to community control over its food. The group started a store, warehouse, trucking company and bakery under the name Red Clover Workers' Brigade. Later the bakery separated from the group and, after a number of changes, began life as Alvarado Street Bakery.

Today, the business grosses more than $7 million a year and employs 110 people. It operates a modern 20,000-square-foot production facility in the college town of Rohnert Park in California's Sonoma County. The bakery and bagel production lines start up at 5 a.m., with the bakery line closing at 8 p.m. and the bagel line closing at 10 p.m. The facility operates six days a week, producing daily averages of more than 11,000 loaves and 4,000 bagels.

Originally, Alvarado Street distributed its products to the natural food shops and co-ops that dot the communities of northern California. As the quality and name of its product grew, a wider market opened up. Alvarado Street's products are now found in most major chains and many independent grocery stores in northern California. The bakery operates about 20 regular delivery routes in the region, five days a week, distributing out of the Sonoma facility and a Sacramento depot. Recently, the bakery added a freezer facility to enhance sales of frozen bakery products. As a result, it's added a freezer truck run to southern California and opened up regular frozen sales to the east and southeast United States.

With more production and distribution capacity available, Alvarado Street has turned to radio advertising to increase sales. Since 1990, the bakery has advertised on some of the largest stations in northern California. The strategy has paid off, leading to increased consumer awareness and higher sales, as well as establishing Alvarado Street as a major player among retailers. The radio presence also has transformed the "hippie bakery" image. Indeed, if you could see the active production facility and the trucks streaming out of the loading docks, you'd have to admit these hippies are going places.

Like other fast-growing companies, the bakery has gone through many changes to get to where it is today. For more than a decade, the bakery operated with a very informal structure. It held monthly membership meetings at which all decisions were made. "Often there were 45 people sitting around on the floor keenly discussing every detail of our business," Gierkout remembers. Understandably, meetings were often lengthy. Standing committees composed of three or four members made the day-to-day decisions about the bakery's production, distribution and financing. Notwithstanding the awkward structure, the members' commitment to their organic line of bakery goods continued to drive the organization's growth.

But by the end of the 1980s, it was clear that the co-op's informal, direct decision-making structure was no longer capable of keeping up with the growth. Since then a number of changes have been made that have maintained the co-op model, yet streamlined its effectiveness.

To become a co-op member, you must have worked at the bakery for nine months. Because the bakery is in a college community, turnover is high and many employees don't reach the nine-month stage. Members must invest in one "A" (voting) share of the co-op. The $1,000 share may be purchased outright, or the co-op will lay out the money for purchase of the share and deduct $4.61 per week from the worker's paycheck until the $1,000 is repaid. Of the present 110 employees, 48 are members and 62 are not.

Members elect a nine-member board that meets monthly. All members may attend board meetings. The board hires a general coordinator who's in charge of the various department heads. At the annual membership meeting, the board presents a budget and business plan to members for approval or modification. In addition, quarterly membership meetings are held at which members can participate in discussion on a wide range of issues.

Any profits above that needed for the business are shared equally among the members. A gain-sharing bonus, paid quarterly, kicks in when profits reach 5 percent above projections. All member dividends are based on hours worked, not pay levels. For each hour worked each year, the member gets one additional "B" share credited to his or her account. ("A" shares are a single share that gives the worker member voting rights.) Members generally receive about 15 percent to 20 percent more income than nonmembers. When a worker-member leaves the co-op, the shares earned are paid back over three years. Thus, the worker-driven environment has a number of pluses and a great deal of flexibility, which add up to low absentee rates.

One of the bakery's limitations is access to capital. At this time its only equity capital comes from members' shares and retained earnings. Like most cooperatives, Alvarado Street is conservative about borrowing. Internal capital has fueled most of the bakery's growth. As a result, the co-op has grown slower than demand and is not always able to purchase the equipment it needs. On the other hand, managing the growth has ensured that Alvarado Street hasn't expanded so fast it would need to sell out. Also, slow growth has kept the bakery focused on the co-op structure as the preferred way of doing business.

Although the various changes described above have brought about a more effective organization and higher productivity, the co-op realizes it must continue to pay attention to higher salaries for management positions. As the co-op has grown, it's required more competence and professional capacity to run it. Attracting and keeping management-level staff is essential to Alvarado Street's success. Yet, higher pay for some must be balanced with the egalitarian nature of the organization. As the cooperative has grown, so has its capacity to make the changes essential for its future. The journey has not been without its problems, but there always has been progress.

Alvarado Street Bakery stands as a strong example of a group of people who discovered that a cooperative is the best organizational form for supporting their practices and philosophy. No organization focused solely on profit would have dared to be a pioneer in the organic baking industry. It was the co-op's commitment to quality products and to an egalitarian structure that allowed Alvarado Street to perfect itself as a bakery and as a cooperative. That's why it's now the nation's largest cooperative bakery and the largest organic bakery.

Incidentally, visitors often wonder about the bakery's name, considering that it's not on Alvarado Street. Hanging over one of the bakery's ovens is a street sign proclaiming "Alvarado Street" – a memento from the co-op's early days. Back then, a driver once fell asleep at the wheel picking up supplies in southern California. He crashed into the sign, not injuring himself and only scratching up the truck. But, worried about the cost of the damaged sign, he threw it into the back of his truck and returned to the bakery, with the sign in tow, to tell his story. Hence the name. Indeed, since that day the Alvarado Street Bakery has crashed through many barriers on its way to becoming an industry pacesetter.

BOOKPEOPLE: FROM COUNTERCULTURE TO INDUSTRY LEADER

These titles probably sound familiar: **Whole Earth Catalog, Trout Fishing in America, How to Keep Your Volkswagen Alive.** Those titles may take you back to the 1960s and '70s, conjuring up images of flower children and love beads. But for a small distributing company called Bookpeople, those titles were the mother's milk of the unique enterprise they began in 1968 in Berkeley, CA, the capital of alternative America.

Begun as a small, private company distributing trade paperbacks, from the beginning Bookpeople showed a special interest in small-press literature. With the plethora of titles emerging from the burgeoning alternative press, Bookpeople's business boomed. In 1969, **Trout Fishing in America** became the company's first success with sales of more than 1,000 copies a week. At about the same time, Stewart Brand gave Bookpeople the exclusive right to distribute the **Whole Earth Catalog**. The first printing in the fall of 1968 was 2,000; the reprinting a year later jumped to 160,000.

The success that came with distributing such hits set the tenor for Bookpeople and paid for their move to a larger warehouse in 1971. That year, the firm won the exclusive right to distribute **How to Keep Your Volkswagen Alive.** After being reviewed in *Life* magazine, the book's sales hit 120,000 in its first year. Once again, Bookpeople had the foresight to channel the cash flow into improving the business, this time by purchasing a computer system.

During this time, Bookpeople grew considerably; it now operated a publishing division (Bookworks) and a distributing arm (Bookpeople). Many of the employees felt that the owners were too involved in the publishing efforts, thus neglecting the distribution aspect. A schism developed between owners and employees.

Perhaps "employees" isn't the correct term. What was attractive about working for Bookpeople was that it portrayed itself as a community in search of cultural change. The people who worked there, many of them bookish long-hairs, were activists in the Cultural Revolution. In their view, Bookpeople wasn't actually "owned" by anyone; it was owned by all of them. In effect, the company was an anarchist commune following the practices of the books it sold, such as Ernest Callenbach's **Ecotopia** , where all the firms are worker-owned. In this case, to borrow a phrase from Marshall McLuhan, "You are what you read."

In 1971, the owners called a meeting to inform employees that they were bringing in efficiency experts to "hover over their hippie heads" and clock their work. After lunch on the day of the evaluations the names of all the employees were read over the public address system, informing them they were being fired for nonperformance. By the end of the afternoon, the employees had stashed anything of value into unmarked boxes and deposited them at the back of the warehouse. The company couldn't conduct its business, and all employees were either on strike or fired – depending on whom you asked.

Days later, the owners realized there was no future for them and offered to sell the business to the strikers. Scrounging up $500 each and putting together a loan agreement, the long-hairs bought the company. In most companies, a change in ownership means firings, speedups and intrigue among management. At Bookpeople, Christmas had come to the commune. The pressure was off, the tension was gone, and drugs and free love continued to be part of everyday life at the enterprise. The employees made the rules, and the first rule was that no one was to rule. The last question on the employment application asked irreverently: "Have you ever lived in Walnut Creek?" – referring to the nearby commuter suburb that was the antithesis to the countercultural life lived by Bookpeople's employee-owners.

What would save Bookpeople from eventual suicide was the workers' unswerving commitment to meeting the needs of northern California's many small yet powerful bookstores. Bookpeople knew this community like a friend. It had been with them through thick and thin and had always been ahead of the pack in unearthing the new masterpieces of the era. If something was changing, Bookpeople discovered it first. If a trend was developing, Bookpeople spotted it first. The small-press surge was to take the organization through many crises, but it too would run its course.

If it was to survive as a distributor, Bookpeople needed to get into the mass market. Until 1971, mass-market books could only be ordered through magazine distributors. After a number of unsuccessful tries, Bookpeople finally broke through the barrier. The key was that Bookpeople had created a unique distribution network that sold many books. The mass market needed an entree, and Bookpeople would be the Pony Express that would take mass-market books where they'd never gone before.

The marriage worked, but it meant that the people at Bookpeople had to work harder and smarter. The new workers coming in were similar in culture, but they brought new competencies. Clashes arose between those who saw the need for some form of hierarchy and management structure, and those who wanted things to stay as loose as they'd always been. Other disputes cropped up over pay levels related to contribution. Pay at Bookpeople went up based only on length of service. (Even today, most wages are tenure-based.) People who really were managers had no chance of receiving appropriate compensation. Although many loved the company, it was getting harder for experienced employees to pass up job offers from the outside world.

Gene Taback, a long-time worker and one-time company president, describes the situation at the time: "In the counterculture it was thought that a lack of authority would promote good will. In fact, the opposite often happened. It drove people away because when there were problems, there was no way to resolve them."

By the mid-1970s, something had to be done. The recession had put an end to the growth pattern, and the internal tensions continued to rise. One by one all of the people who had been part of the original buyout had left. Bookpeople was also losing its exclusive distributing contracts; with the departure of the **Whole Earth Catalog,** there were none. Bookpeople had to start all over again.

Out went all books that seemed never to move, including great classics of literature. In came the next stage of a solution: the catalog. Gathered into one big book was the most esoteric collection of titles that ever fit between two covers of a book distributors catalog. Bookpeople had done it again – surprising the trade with its innovation and astounding the inland booksellers with the access to hitherto unknown titles that were taking Pacific Coast readers by storm. Once again, Bookpeople had surfed to the edge of the wave and somehow navigated around the rocks. That's been the story for almost 30 years and, given the company's bent for metamorphism, it may be the story for years to come. Perhaps no company has changed so much and continued to lead.

Today, Bookpeople is owned by the Bookpeople Employees Association and incorporated under California's for-profit laws. It regards itself as an employee-owned corporation. After six months of employment, an employee must become an owner. At present there are 90 full-time employees, 75 of whom are owner-members. An employee can either buy 50 shares at $10 each or have the $500 deducted over time from his or her paycheck. Either way, each owner is required to own $500 in shares in the company. From that moment on, employee-owners can vote their shares at all association elections. For example, in board elections an owner can vote all 50 shares for one candidate, or split the shares among several nominees. The owners elect a board of five to run the company. The board of directors hires and fires the general manager and the director of human resources. Employees answer to heads of the 10 different company departments.

Profits at Bookpeople are split equally between retained earnings for the company and bonuses for the employee-owners. However, Bookpeople first pays attention to providing employee benefits, such as free lunches and an excellent health-care plan. The bonuses are based on hours worked and are usually about equal across the board, as most people work a full-time schedule. "Discussion of wage scales is ongoing and enduring at Bookpeople," says Taback, who has been on the board for almost all of his more than 25 years of service.

As a company past president, Taback has a few observations about Bookpeople's employee ownership. The upside, he notes, is that the structure means employee-owners are better informed about the company and more dedicated. As for the downside, he says the company is poorly capitalized, has little motivation to make major business changes and has little reason to incentivize key employees.

Visiting Bookpeople does overwhelm the senses. You enter into a showroom with an amazing array of book titles. Clearly, Bookpeople retains its pioneer status. Then Taback ushers you past throngs of telephone operators dressed in comfortable "new age" clothing. There's an air of metaphysical calm about the place. All the offices are cluttered with books, and all the walls are covered with beautiful posters advertising book fairs or literary events. The phones are ringing, the computers are whirring, and Bookpeople's day goes on. Next, Taback sweeps you back down the carpeted corridor, through a door and into another world: distribution. The rows of books stretch for as far as the eye can see in this 75,000-square-foot storage area. Down every aisle people scurry with book trolleys, filling orders for a book-reading public. Some workers lean against the racks reading what they just picked up. Here and there are hives of activity where the book-runners bring their stash to the packaging department. Into the boxes go the orders, which then get shipped off to a bookstore. If an order comes in by noon, it goes out that day.

It seems that Bookpeople has facilitated two revolutions: one in independent publishing and the other in independent book selling. Like many other worker cooperatives, Bookpeople discovered a niche because its owners were committed to the product of their operation, as well as to the structure of their enterprise. The form of organization wasn't driven by profit on shares but by a choice of lifestyle and a community. Surely, Bookpeople has mellowed over the years, but it hasn't lost its verve to be vanguards in the book-distributing world. The $500 dollars each employee put in 30 years ago was the beginning of a company that now does $25 million in sales a year. Any way you look at it, that's no small change for revolutionaries.

CONCLUSION

Worker cooperatives have popped up in numerous industries, in various sectors of society. Some of these enterprises had countercultural roots, with their founders looking for a more humane, egalitarian – even "laid-back" – work environment. Other worker-owned ventures have offered a pathway out of poverty for people in traditionally low-paying jobs. Still others have sprung up at times of company ownership changes, when the workers saw self-ownership as a way to take control and safeguard their jobs.

Whatever the initial motivations may have been, worker-owned companies clearly offer many benefits to those who work in them. But it isn't just the worker-owners who stand to gain. Many companies are realizing that in today's climate, with people desiring more out of their jobs than just a paycheck, worker ownership is a way to give people a genuine feeling of involvement in their workplace. Perhaps nothing is more motivating on the job than having a say in how things get done and a personal stake in the outcomes. That kind of involvement is a powerful antidote to the apathy and absenteeism plaguing many companies today.

ACKNOWLEDGMENTS
Michael Gierkout, President, Alvarado Street Bakery, Rohnert Park, CA
Joseph Tuck, Alvarado Street Bakery, Rohnert Park, CA
Rick Surpin, President, Cooperative Home Care Associates, Bronx, NY
Eugene Taback, President, Bookpeople Employee Assoc., Inc., Oakland, CA

REFERENCES AND SOURCES
Marks, Laurie. 1987. "Outward Bound." *East Bay Express.* January 9: 9-13.
Pacyniak, Bernard. 1991. "An Organic Offshoot." *Bakery.* June: 120-131.

PART II:
MEETING HUMAN NEEDS
COOPERATIVELY

CHAPTER 5.

COOPERATIVE HOUSING BRINGS THE DREAM HOME

For many Americans of modest financial means, the dream of home ownership has come to seem out of reach in recent years. Even so, one way that dream is being kept alive for many people is through cooperative ownership of their homes.

Nearly 150 years ago, housing co-ops began to appear in New York City as an answer to the working person's search for affordable housing. New York City is now this nation's hotbed of co-op housing activity, for rich and poor New Yorkers alike.

Today, cooperative housing is a nationwide phenomenon. This chapter will look at the struggles and successes of various New York projects over the decades, as well as at two housing co-ops in other parts of the United States.

ONE IN A MILLION

For Rossana Perez, the prospects of home ownership seemed gloomy indeed. As a single mother raising two children, she lives in Los Angeles, where $200,000 is the median price for a house, and where only 40 percent of the population own their own homes, compared to a 60 percent national average.

Still, Perez beat the odds stacked against her. Today she and her two children live in a two-bedroom house in the 66-unit Marathon Housing Co-op in Los Angeles. Marathon is a housing co-op that stretches eleven blocks and is composed of single family homes, duplexes and triplexes. She was able to buy her co-op share for $500, for a house in a neighborhood where homes start at around $250,000. With the help of a subsidy from the Department of Housing and Urban Development (HUD), her monthly rent is only $350, half of what she'd pay for a house half the size of the one she owns.

Perez is glad her days of apartment-renter transience and landlord hassles are over. More importantly, she has a community of support all around her. Fellow co-op owners assist her in her efforts to raise two children alone. That's especially crucial to Perez because she's active in community work in Los Angeles, as well as in her home country of El Salvador, and needs to be away from home fairly often. She needs good neighbors – and she has them.

In return, those neighbors recognize Perez's gifts: her understanding, empathy, excellent bilingual communication skills (she's also a published poet) and leadership abilities. In May 1995, two years after she moved into the co-op, her neighbors elected her as the co-op's president. "It's a big task," Perez says of her position, "and a lot of work. However, the co-op is in good shape, there are three working committees, and we have high participation from our members."

Before buying into Marathon, Perez knew about the people-helping-people benefits of co-ops from her work in El Salvador. These days, when she tells others she lives in a co-op, she often encounters misperceptions. Many think of a housing co-op as being a sort of commune, where residents each have their own rooms and share meals together. Perez takes time to explain the housing co-op idea – that she is an owner, has her own apartment, that residents are in control of their own housing, and that they elect a board of directors from their own ranks to take care of the co-op's business affairs.

In turn, Perez says she's learned a lot from her co-op involvement. "Organizing takes a lot of time," she observes, "and you need to be open to other people's ideas. People need to know that you're listening to them. You must start from respecting the other person's opinion. Empowering people is a long process that requires patience."

As Perez sees it, not only is the co-op providing affordable housing to her family and her neighbors. It's a step toward better understanding among people of varying cultural and language backgrounds. "It's critical," she says, "that we understand how to live in harmony."

Perez and her two children comprise one of the roughly 1 million American families now living in housing co-ops, according to the National Association of Housing Cooperatives in Alexandria, Va. Of the current number of housing units, one-third are specifically targeted for low- or moderate-income families, while the remainder are privately financed at market rates.

COOPERATIVE LIVING THROUGH THE AGES

Some observers trace the roots of co-op housing in this country back to a thousand years ago, when the Anasazi Indians built their apartment-like pueblos into the cliffs throughout the southwest U.S. canyon country. Certainly, with their communal ownership, the Anasazi created an early form of co-op housing, of sorts. But did they operate on the principle of one vote per housing unit? Did they elect a board of directors? History hasn't answered such questions.

The modern co-op housing movement had its start, however, in the concrete canyons of New York City in the mid-19th century (we'll look at this in detail in the next section of this chapter).

Another spurt in co-op housing development in this country occurred in the 1930s, with the emergence of student housing cooperatives at several universities. Today more than 165 such co-ops are still in existence, serving as affordable "homes away from home" for some 10,000 college students nationwide. What's more, these co-ops give students hands-on learning opportunities in housing management, finance and democratic decision-making.

Student co-ops in both the United States and Canada belong to the North American Students of Cooperation, based in Ann Arbor, MI NASCO provides guidance and development services to the student cooperative community, with NASCO's annual conference serving as an energetic gathering site for student co-op leaders.

The 1950s ushered in another era of massive cooperative housing development throughout the United States, thanks to passage of Section 213 of the National Housing Act. To this day, co-ops organized under Section 213 claim the lowest default rate of any HUD multifamily program.

The fervor of the 1950s faded considerably by the 1970s, as government sources of co-op financing dried up. New sources have emerged, however, in the form of affordable housing programs at the state level and through regional financial institutions and foundations.

The 1980s saw the advent of banks making loans directly to housing cooperatives, largely spurred by the growing role of cooperatives in apartment conversions. Apartment conversion activity – that is, converting apartment buildings to condominiums and cooperatives – sprang up in the 1970s. By the next decade, cities had begun to grapple with the issue of long-term renter displacement resulting from condominium conversions. In many cities, owner-occupied cooperatives came to be viewed as an effective way to protect renters. Consequently, more than half of all apartment conversions since 1982 have been to cooperatives.

A newer surge of interest in co-ops has been fed by the growing interest during the past two decades in a concept known as "New Urbanism," with its focus on bringing back neighborhood relationships and rebuilding community. Cooperative housing has been a natural fit in the New Urbanism philosophy. One form of this is CoHousing, a Danish concept that is now being put into action by more than 150 groups in the United States. The CoHousing model is based on residents living in their own units, but also committing to participating in community activities, such as eating together in a "common house." Residents own their own homes, but also have a shared interest in the common house and other common areas.

NEW YORK CITY: CO-OP HOUSING'S BIRTHPLACE IN THE UNITED STATES

To millions of people around the world, New York City evokes images of towering skyscrapers, a city that never sleeps, where the pampered elite live just moments away from unconscionable poverty. Television and motion pictures have captured the excitement of New York City life, even for those of us who'll never experience it. Yet, when the camera pans across the fabled Manhattan skyline, it also captures in its eye one of the most important co-op movements in the United States: the housing co-ops of New York City. Today nearly 2 million New Yorkers live in 600,000 housing co-op units, which account for more than half of the total number of co-op units in this country.

Cooperative housing in New York meets many needs for all levels of income groups. Low-income service workers and millionaire stockbrokers in the canyons of Wall Street both go home to their housing co-ops. There are luxury cooperatives that sell for millions at market price, as well as low- and moderate-income cooperatives affordable to the rest of us. The common theme of housing co-ops is ownership, responsibility and a democratic organization.

How did a community-oriented idea formulated in Rochdale, England, in the revolutionary times of 1844 become the most popular form of home ownership in the heart of American capitalism? Attribute much of it to geography. A city that began on the narrow granite island of Manhattan had to build upwards to house its people. To find the capital to finance the growth, developers adopted cooperative ownership as the main way to give residents a stake.

Some housing cooperative historians give credit for developing the first true housing co-op in the United States to a group of Finnish workers in Brooklyn. In 1916, they formed the Finnish Home Building Association, based on "one member, one vote," and built an apartment-style co-op named Alku 1. Alku is the Finnish word for beginning, and the co-op truly was just that. By 1926, there were 25 other Finnish housing co-ops in the Sunset Park area of Brooklyn, a Finnish enclave for those arriving by boat from the mother country.

The first recorded form of cooperative housing in New York City, however, was an artist's cooperative built in 1857 to provide studios, galleries and living space for its members. Twenty years later, Felix Adler, founder of the Ethical Culture Society, helped fund a model tenement run as a cooperative. In frequent touch with British co-op leaders, Adler was a major sponsor of a speaking tour of the United States by the well-known British co-op champion, George Jacob

Holyoake. Holyoake used the pulpits in New York to recount the myriad successes of the growing British cooperative movement. Adler and others applied this new-found fervor to their efforts to provide better housing communities in New York City. The co-op idea imported from Europe merged with the new multistory housing models being developed in New York.

There, the earliest defined cooperative housing project was the Randolph, a hotel apartment built in 1876. With the development of new building techniques and, in particular, the elevator, there followed a number of similar high-rise housing co-ops in Manhattan. They provided quality housing with shared services and facilities for higher income families. From that era on, the co-op form of ownership has continued to be the most popular form of housing in Manhattan.

The ideas emerging in the early 1900s from the Garden City Movement started by Ebenezer Howard in England impacted a number of innovative New York housing developers. Many of these projects blended the good planning and open space of a Garden City suburb with the cooperative ownership model. As a result, the New York City region now has some of the most admired and attractive apartment communities in the world.

During the same period, the Rockefeller family played a unique role in developing co-op housing in New York. They funded the 170-unit Thomas Gardens, one of the first moderate-income co-ops. Because this was in an era of segregated housing, Thomas Garden's residents were all white. Recognizing their responsibility to build an equal model for nonwhites, the Rockefellers then funded the first all-black housing cooperative, the 511-unit Laurence Dunbar Apartments in Harlem.

For a time during the 1930s there was an exciting utopian era in New York. Progressive and ethnic Jewish groups built a number of experimental cooperative housing communities there. These were extensive efforts to build models of a new society in what appeared to be the crumbling demise of capitalism. Rich in traditions and imbued with a vision of creating heaven on earth, these activists set out to change the world. A number of large housing co-ops became centers of radical thought, culture and action.

The size of their planned communities and the inspiring architecture were a tribute to common people in pursuit of their dreams. Gathered in strength and solidarity, they intended to build a new world or a new Jerusalem. However, the Depression that spurred them on would also to be their downfall. Their principles were challenged by the poverty and drastic unemployment of the era. Finding it difficult to evict nonpaying members, the co-ops fell behind on their mortgages. While many residents waited for the revolution to come, the banks waited for the rent. Thus, the radicals were put in the position of being landlords.

Hating their role, they could neither collect the rents nor evict their friends, and the co-ops fell even further behind on their mortgages. Soon thereafter, the banks, whom the co-ops blamed for the worldwide economic slump, also repossessed the co-ops' dreams.

Fortunately, a co-op model created in the late 1920s by the Amalgamated Clothing Workers Union of America did succeed. Through tough leadership, the "Amalgamated," as it was called, chose the hard path of reality over the rocky road of idealism. No matter how difficult, they made sure they paid the mortgage every month. When the Depression ended, the co-op model was alive, and the members of the 1,400-unit co-op in the Bronx were ready to tell their story of unity in community. Ordinary working people had triumphed and secured their own model of cooperative housing. A new era was about to unfold through the efforts of Amalgamated Union's leaders, Sidney Hillman, Jacob S. Potofsky and Abraham E. Kazan.

The other unions listened to Amalgamated, and in 1951 they formed the United Housing Foundation (UHF) to sponsor low- and moderate-income co-op housing throughout New York City. For the next 50 years, the New York City-based trade unions became the cooperative housing leaders in this country. In 1965, UHF reached a new pinnacle when they built the 5,860-unit Rochdale Village. Named after the town in England where the first co-op store began in 1844, it's now the second largest housing co-op in the United States.

Union-sponsored co-op housing reached its greatest height when Co-op City opened in the Bronx in 1972. With its 15,382 units and almost 50,000 residents, it's a new city that owes the single largest housing mortgage in the world. Co-op City has its own schools, shopping centers, power plant, post offices, places of worship, office buildings and police force. When it opened, New York Governor Nelson Rockefeller heralded Co-op City as the most powerful tool New York had ever assembled to provide affordable housing.

With Co-op City completed, UHF had built scores of projects and nearly 50,000 co-op units in a scant 20 years. In almost all cases, the housing co-ops were cities within a city. Many had their own co-op stores, credit unions and co-op child care. For the visionary co-op and union leaders, it was a challenging yet pensive moment. Although they had seen their radical ideals fade, they had witnessed their reforms succeed. These ordinary men and women had altered forever the New York City skyline.

Since the early 1970s, government financing for all forms of housing has slowed to a trickle. UHF went from a thriving powerhouse in New York City to an organization in search of a new role. Fortunately, the passing of time provided new opportunities, such as developing NORC (naturally occurring retirement communities) projects. The NORC model began with Penn South. This cooperative of 2,820 units is at the forefront of a major issue facing many housing co-ops in New York City. Most of Penn South's residents are aging in place; 5,000 of the 6,500 residents are seniors, and many live alone. The leadership at Penn South is implementing an activist, on-site, multiservice program that supports continued independence of the residents. At the Penn South Program for Seniors, more than 300 seniors receive ongoing health and social service assistance each month. The NORC program intends to find the best way for New York's housing co-ops to manage this demographic change. (See chapter on senior housing co-ops.)

The co-op housing birthplace continues to be a thriving scene today. Whether it be for workers or retirees, young or old, low-income or high-income, New York City's co-ops are still creating home-ownership opportunities.

WHERE A FREEWAY MIGHT HAVE BEEN

Back on the other side of the country, far from Manhattan's skyscrapers, Rossana Perez and her neighbors are reaping the benefits of co-op living in the sprawling environment of Los Angeles. Here a housing co-op opportunity emerged out of an urban planning problem. Between 1960 and 1975, the California Division of Highways (later known as Caltrans) bought up parcels of land along a strip a block wide and more than two miles long in the Echo Park/Silverlake neighborhood, targeting the area for a future freeway to be known as Route 2. But when the freeway boom faded, Route 2 was canceled, and Caltrans had land on its hands to sell.

For Caltrans it was just a sign of the times and a simple decision. But for the approximately 1,500 people who lived in the 544 housing units now owned by Caltrans, life was about to change dramatically. Because of the mixture of single-family homes, duplexes, triplexes and apartment buildings, proposals abounded for how Caltrans should sell off the properties. In particular, renters of the single-family homes wanted a first right of refusal to buy. The complexities of the situation unfortunately slowed down the process. Negotiating took place at a time when real estate prices for the area saw some home values increase by 50 percent from 1975 to 1977.

The concerns of Route 2 residents reached new heights daily with every new report of the increased value of housing in the area. They held community meetings and formed the Route 2 Tenants Association (R2TA). Though a majority of the parcels were occupied by single-family dwellings (120 out of 200), the early agreement was "one for all and all for one." Whatever the plan, it would have to accommodate every single inhabitant of all the existing housing units. The residents' unity and their effective publicity won immediate support from their local state senator, a powerful figure in Sacramento. The resident's show of force also gained them support from the attorney general's office, which ruled that the units could be disposed of by Caltrans at below market value. This ruling was soon augmented by state legislation.

But the struggle was far from over. The question now arose as to what to do next. Several proposals surfaced. One of these was to convert to a cooperative ownership plan, which would qualify the residents for rent subsidies. Many residents who owned single-family homes, however, opposed this idea. As a result, the legislation ultimately was divided into two parts – one for single-family units and the other for multifamily units.

More obstacles cropped up in the ensuing years, among them legal hurdles, political maneuverings, a roller coaster real estate market, lack of financing for the multifamily units, language barriers among the residents and conflicting self-interests. Residents began to burn out, wondering if the process would ever bring any real answers for their housing needs. In the midst of the turmoil, Caltrans, which was still the landlord at this point, raised rents by 10 percent. In response, resident leaders called for a rent strike, a move that 80 percent of the residents supported. Eventually media coverage forced Caltrans to back down. The bureaucrats came across as neglectful landlords, up against a multiethnic coalition of low-income people fighting for their homes.

By 1980, the tide began to shift from protests to possibilities. The residents' development organization received its first funding from the city of Los Angeles. Community development block grants were channeled into forming a development corporation, and additional funding came in from the state. The board of the residents' organization also transformed itself from a self-appointed body to a federation of co-op representatives, as it had been decided that each major apartment building would become a separate cooperative.

Finding a lender to be a partner in the development process was the next hurdle. Banks generally wanted nothing to do with the project. But eventually the Savings Association Mortgage Company (SAMCO) agreed to finance two buildings. SAMCO, which was set up by the savings and loan associations in California to finance low-income housing, is one of the most innovative lenders in the state. With SAMCO on board, the rest of the lending community began to get involved.

With acceptance of the limited equity co-op model in place and financing assured, the first stage was complete. The next stage was the hardest, as in-fighting developed. The Latino residents found their voice, and government agencies took a harder look at the projects. The honeymoon was over, and the residents had to acknowledge that their initial attempt at self-management had failed. The projects needed managing, and protesters have not always made good managers. In the sobering aftermath of struggle, the resident owners slowly took control away from the interest-group leadership.

Finally, the residents placed their focus on making the co-ops work. Thus, the legacy of a canceled freeway project is now a string of five affiliated scattered-site housing co-ops providing 272 homes for people in the Echo Park/Silverlake neighborhood. People can buy into one of the co-ops for a down payment as low as $300. Two-thirds of the units' owners receive HUD low-income subsidies, which bring the average monthly rent down to $262. Vacancies are few, and turnover is limited.

At the Route 2 site, rental housing and disgruntled tenants have been replaced by cooperatives whose residents now control their lives. Alienation is being changed through association. Working class families, mainly Latino, are breaking down barriers and rebuilding community.

Allan Heskin, a UCLA professor of urban planning who has documented the project's long struggle in his book, **The Struggle for Community,** is enthusiastic about the progress made at Route 2. "It re-creates the neighborhoods of the past where everyone knows everyone," Heskin notes. "There is a sense of power through participation that people never had before. You get to know you control the co-op through acting like a member. It's the closest thing to grass roots democracy I have ever seen."

"If you want community-building," Heskin adds, "this is it. We organize to give people control over their lives. People who normally have no say in their lives have a say in the co-ops. Democracy for most working people is harsh and often an enemy, whereas democracy within the co-ops is a tool and the only way to build our future."

STUDIO TAKEOVER IN BOSTON

Yet another example of people taking control of their housing – and their lives – is found in Boston, MA, at the Fenway Studios. Built in 1905, the 46-unit Fenway Studios project was a model of the noblesse oblige of the era. It was designed to be made up of artists' live-work studios, with the front studio workspace having a high ceiling and large north-facing windows. In consultation with the leading painters of the era living in Boston, the interior design was copied from the Paris ateliers where many of them had studied. The architects, Parker and Thomas, designed the exterior after aspects of the Arts and Crafts Movement from Britain.

The location was chosen due to its proximity to newly built institutions, such as Symphony Hall (1900), the New England Conservatory of Music (1902) and the Museum of Fine Arts, then under construction. Local art patrons bought shares in the Fenway Studios Trust, which was created to construct and manage the building. The original sponsors were a "who's who" of Boston society. Since inception, Fenway Studios has been the "Mecca" for key figures in Boston's art society. In recognition of its architectural and historical significance, Fenway Studios was listed in the National Register of Historic Buildings in 1978.

The year before that the descendants of the original owners had been under intense pressure to sell the property. To prevent the building being converted into high-priced condominiums, the residents organized "Artists for the Preservation of the Fenway Studios." They hired a consultant, lined up investors and purchased an option on the property. But efforts to obtain permanent financing seemed impossible. Financial institutions didn't understand cooperatives or trust artists. But in the nick of time, a light appeared on the horizon. Congress created the National Cooperative Bank (NCB) in 1980 to provide funding for just such unique borrowers. With its understanding of cooperative structures and a healthy infusion of federal funds, NCB was able to fund the Fenway Studios purchase. By December 1981, the resident artists were celebrating their cooperative ownership. Since then they have made extensive renovations and repairs to the building. It's home, and they intend to take care of it.

Fenway Studios is now a stable cooperative and one of the focal points of the Boston arts community. It's one of the few places in Boston where artists can find affordable home ownership, a purpose-built live-work studio and a built-in community of fellow artists. Only visual artists and their families approved by the board may own and occupy the units. More than 30 artists desiring to live at Fenway are now on the waiting list. Because it's now an affordable cooperative, turnover is very low. When the sale of a co-op membership does occur, there's a limit on the appreciation the seller receives. Using this method guarantees permanent affordability to future artist residents.

The residents of Fenway Studios are proud of their past, yet even more passionate about their future. They want to build a better cooperative not only for themselves, but also for artists in the future. They see themselves as stewards of a legacy created for Boston's fine arts community. They're part of an American tradition that has looked for ways to house artists within a community. The earliest of such efforts was the 10th Street Studio in New York City, built in 1857 by arts patron James Boorman Johnson. Today all across the country, artists are coming together to build similar cooperatives, with the Twin Cities of Minneapolis/St. Paul leading the way in supporting artists' communities.

For too many artists, however, the community models are too few. Housing is transient, good studios hard to find, and home and work usually isolated from each other. Living on the margin of society might create a few good, yet troubled artists. But most, like Teri Malo, do their best work when they don't have to worry about the rent.

Malo moved to Fenway Studios with her family when the co-op was formed. In her airy studio, she paints tropical watercolors based on images from a recent visit to Costa Rica. The light and artists' ambiance at Fenway Studios bring out the best in her. The tall walls are covered with her work. In her colorful kitchen, with the south light streaming in and a good cup of coffee in her hand, she talks about the co-op's value to her. "I have a home, a place to paint and an artists' community with which to interact," she says. "As an artist living in the city, it's hard to find stability. I have all of those elements here at Fenway."

CONCLUSION

Whether it's student housing co-ops on this nation's college campuses, cooperatively owned apartments amidst Los Angeles' urban sprawl, or live-work artists' studios in historic Boston buildings, housing cooperatives offer people from all walks of life, of all income groups, a means of gaining control over their housing. Housing co-ops translate into home ownership opportunities for many Americans who might not otherwise be able to afford their own homes.

As we have seen in this chapter, the routes to housing co-op formation can be diverse. Legal, financial and philosophical struggles sometimes crop up along the way. But as housing costs in this country continue to spiral out of sight, housing cooperatives may deserve greater attention. For many people, housing co-ops may be one key strategy for keeping the dream of home ownership within reach.

ACKNOWLEDGMENTS

David Freed, Vice President, National Cooperative Bank Development Corporation, Washington D.C.

Allan David Heskin, Professor, UCLA Urban Planning Program, Los Angeles, CA

Herb Levy, Executive Director, National Assoc. of Housing Cooperatives, Alexandria, Va.

Teri Malo, Board Member, Fenway Studios, Inc., Boston, MA

Rosanna Perez, President, Route 2 Co-op, Los Angeles, CA

Allen Thurgood, Executive Director, Co-ordinating Council for Cooperatives, New York, NY

Ed Yaker, President, Amalgamated Housing Co-op, Bronx, NY

REFERENCES AND SOURCES

Heskin, Allan David. 1991. **The Struggle for Community**. Boulder, Colo.: Westview Press.

Karp, Naomi J. 1994. **Cooperative and Condominium Housing in New York City**. New York: Action Committee for Reasonable Real Estate Taxes.

CHAPTER 6.

SENIOR CO-OP HOUSING:
FOCUSING ON COMMUNITY, HEALTH CARE & SERVICES

*The senior years are a life-phase filled with transitions –
physiological, psychological and financial. While upper-class senior
citizens have multiple choices available to them as to where and how to
live in their retirement years, the options are fewer for seniors of
modest means. No longer being wage-earners and now faced with
getting by on fixed economic resources, many seniors worry about
being able to continue to afford to pay their living expenses. A sizable
portion of these are related to housing costs. Rising rents, home
maintenance expenses and property tax increases hit everyone's wallet.
But no one feels them quite as hard as do middle- and low-income
senior citizens.*

*New housing solutions are emerging that offer affordable,
comfortable, community-oriented living arrangements for seniors.
Housing co-ops specifically tailored to meet seniors' needs are a
popular option. This chapter explores four projects involving different
types of housing in vastly different environments. All, however, share
one goal: to give their senior members a place to call home, where
they continue to feel they are in charge of their lives.*

FREEDOM FIGHTERS: SENIORS TAKE CONTROL OF THEIR HOUSING

The mood was tense in the City Council chambers in the small rural
town of Woodland, CA. The room was packed to overflowing with irate
senior citizens from the nearby Leisureville Mobile Home Park. The
source of their anger and frustration was a one-sentence notice they'd
each recently received from their landlord, informing them that in 60
days their rents would be raised by 11 percent, or about $31 dollars per
month per mobile home.

For the nearly 200 Leisureville seniors, the news was terrifying. Most were on fixed incomes, and more than half were low or very low-income. Up to this point, life had been smooth, with rent increases moving up with the consumer price index. But 11 percent was a big jump. And now questions abounded: Where would that extra $31 dollars come from? What would they have to cut in an already marginal budget? Were they trapped by the reality of owning their mobile home, but renting the ground under it from a landlord? How many of them at their age could move their homes? Would they just have to grin and bear it, or could they put up a fight?

A group from Leisureville organized the residents to attend the City Council meeting. Many were known figures in the small farming community who knew how to get things done. Using those skills, the Leisureville organizers were determined to put on a good show. They'd leafleted the park, put together car pools and stirred things up. As a first step, they'd asked the City Council to adopt a rent stabilization ordinance for mobile home parks. They'd called all the Council members and talked to the local press. They were ready, they were organized and were they mad.

Woodland Mayor Elaine Rominger called the meeting to order, looked out over the sea of seniors and wondered how the evening would go. She decided to bring up the Leisureville issue immediately. The speakers representing the park residents were cheered and applauded; the remarks of the landlord's representative were met with stone silence. There was no give or take; solutions took a back seat to the confrontation. Council members were not prepared to take immediate action, even though they sympathized with the seniors. Mayor Rominger appointed Vice-Mayor Gary Sandy to try to mediate an acceptable rent increase between the parties. Relieved by the Council's support and convinced that Sandy was in their corner, the seniors applauded the offer. Still, residents went home not knowing what would happen next. Many still feared they'd have to leave the park.

Little did they know that two years later they would own the park. What happened in between is a saga of seniors on a mission.

At the conclusion of the difficult and contentious negotiations, Leisureville's owner told the residents' committee that if they truly wanted to put an end to the conflict, they should buy the park from him. Without knowing what they were getting into, the residents said yes, they'd buy. From that moment on, they began a two-year journey from renter to resident ownership.

First, the residents formed an unincorporated association and elected a board, which, under the leadership of retired Methodist minister Don Wells, met almost weekly until the sale was complete. The board provided the continuity and competency that saw the park through many difficult periods. "We had everything on our side," Wells says, "motivated residents, a supportive city, competent consultants and a clear path. If we believed, it had to happen." He admits that along the way he often turned to God for inspiration and guidance. "All of us as board members needed to instill confidence in our fellow residents that we would succeed," he notes. "Any display of doubt would have destroyed our efforts."

The board chose a trio of consultants to help arrange the sale, obtain financing and shepherd the residents through the development process. Next the board held a number of community meetings to outline the choices for conversion. A series of newsletters went out to educate the residents of the 150-unit park about resident ownership. The meetings were always well-attended, and interest remained high throughout the process. However, making choices required plenty of information and discussion. These "seasoned citizens" were going to make only good decisions.

Finally, they chose a limited equity cooperative as the structure for the purchase. Each membership would require an investment of $5,000. The residents would continue to own their mobile homes, but they would each hold one share in ownership of the park as a cooperative. Thus, they would own the park together.

One by one their efforts fell into place. The Kaplan Fund of the Cooperative Development Foundation provided predevelopment funds. The three consultants agreed to take their fees only at the close of escrow. The regional Sacramento Presbyterian Foundation gave a grant of $5,000, and the residents put up $3,000 of their own money. The city of Woodland awarded $275,000 in Community Block Grant funds to help the low-income residents purchase their shares in the co-op. The city then sponsored the co-op's winning application in a statewide competition for a HOME award, a program sponsored by the federal government and administered by the individual states. The award to Leisureville was $1 million, the maximum possible. Finally, the owner arranged for the existing low-interest, variable-rate first mortgage to be assumed by the co-op. Then, with $500,000 from Mercy Housing and $300,000 from the Northern California Community Loan Fund in below-market-rate loans and more than $100,000 in loans from residents, the finance package was in place.

Although there had been tense moments during the two years of pulling everything together, the resolve of the residents, the commitment of the city and city staff, and the creativity of the consultants overcame every obstacle. Fortunately, the landlord also forgave a number of deadlines to ensure the co-op's ability to effect the purchase.

In April 1995, the Leisureville community turned out to celebrate their ownership of the park. Sandy, now mayor, complimented the government agencies and financial institutions for playing a role in making this dream come true. Reverend Wells spoke in awe of the difficult journey everyone had taken and the importance of the residents' commitment and sticking together. That morning the room glowed with the feeling that people can shape their own destiny. Against the odds, the seniors of Leisureville had seized control of their lives. Although many were in their 70s and 80s, they'd launched a new era. Through their cooperative, the Leisureville Community Association, they were now proud owners of a park that gave new definition to the meaning of mobile home. That day, just like the Fourth of July, the residents of Leisureville flew the Stars and Stripes from their own homes. They had won their independence.

The first year of ownership was challenging. The board held elections, hired a management company, and then decided not to renew that contract after the first year, but to hire a different management company instead. Also, due to the flat economy in the region, the market for mobile homes was weak. The number of homes for sale in the park rose from 11 to 15. However, the board took all this change in stride, recognizing that this was all part of the co-op's maturing process.

The most important decision the board made in its first year of running the park was to send a letter to all members from the board president on January 24, 1996. At the end of each January, the park residents must be notified of the upcoming year's rent increases. The news was destined to make park residents sit up and take notice. Wells' letter stated, "The board of directors of LCA voted that the LCA members' regular monthly space rent will not be increased this May 1st." Wells added, "I believe you will agree that the 'NO ASSESSMENT INCREASE IS GREAT NEWS!' "

This was the first time since the park was founded in 1976 that the rent hadn't been increased by the owners. The news gained front-page headlines in both local newspapers. After all the work, the door-to-door organizing, the meetings and the park-wide votes, the effort had come down to this. The deal had been structured to benefit the residents, and the results were in. A dream had come true.

The story of Leisureville had a happy ending. Yet for millions of people who live in mobile home parks, the situation is often fraught with fear. Residents own each mobile home, but rent the land it sits on, often on a month-to-month basis or, at best, with a yearly lease. Mobile homes are costly to move and mobile home parks usually don't have empty spaces. Therefore irritating the manager or the owner can bring tremendous repercussions. Owners can raise rents, leaving residents feeling they have no choice but to pay them. Also, owners can sell parks to make way for shopping centers, leaving the mobile home owner out in the cold. Relations between tenants and owners can become bitter. In many states, park owners sponsor legislation to protect their interests. On the other side of the fence are the mobile home residents who, as in California, organize groups such as the Golden State Mobilehome Owners League (GSMOL). To manage the local conflicts, a number of communities have adopted mobile home rent-control ordinances.

In many parts of the United States, especially the northeast (mainly New Hampshire and New York), the South (Florida and Texas) and the West (Arizona, California and Washington), mobile home parks are an important supply of housing. They cost 35 percent less than conventionally constructed housing. Currently, mobile homes (also known as manufactured housing) account for one-third of all single-family homes built in the United States. Because most are built as mobile home parks, they have a significant impact upon the market.

However, they continue to create an underlying tension between the park owner and the mobile home owner who is no more than a tenant. The confrontations that frequently occur have spurred many conversions to resident ownership. Quite often, as was the case at Leisureville, cooperatives arise out of these conversions. Over the past decade, mobile home residents in California bought 100 mobile home parks, with more than 6,000 housing units. Half of these parks adopted the cooperative model. Similar actions are taking place in Florida, where there are more than 200 resident-owned mobile home parks. Because the idea has so much support and makes so much sense, some mobile home communities are now being built from the beginning as cooperatives.

FROM DAIRY TO SENIOR HOUSING CO-OP

Walking into the lobby of a Cooperative Services, Inc. community anywhere in the United States, you will sense the vitality of this senior cooperative housing organization. The strength of CSI is its active resident participation, a pattern that exudes from the grass roots to the top of the organization. From its first co-op apartment building in 1965, CSI committed itself to involving its resident members in the organization's activities and governance. As a result, many cities seek CSI as a development partner. It has a proud record of being one of the most unique and effective senior citizen housing models, and has won many awards in its field.

Today, CSI operates 35 housing co-ops in four states (Michigan, California, Maryland and Massachusetts) and houses almost 5,000 people in more than 4,500 apartment units. Its asset base will soon be $150 million. The co-op's main focus is on providing senior housing at below-market-rate rents.

This successful cooperative began during the Depression. People formed study groups around the country to organize cooperatives and thus conquer their desperate conditions. The 1930s were tough years in Detroit. By the early 1940s, a number of Detroit residents came together, and with $5,500 they incorporated Cooperative Dairy Service, Inc. A decade later, the dairy merged with a retail store, forming a consumer co-op with the name Cooperative Services, Inc. (CSI). CSI then developed a major optical service, which expanded throughout the Detroit area. In 1964, CSI spotted an opportunity to develop cooperative housing for seniors. Finally, in the 1980s, CSI spun off its many different activities as separate cooperatives to concentrate on senior housing. No co-op in America has shed as many skins as CSI before becoming the form of co-op it is today.

However, the origin of CSI arising from the Depression was that of an organization committed to the ideals and practices of cooperation. CSI's founders, and in particular Virginia and Fred Thornthwaite, the long-time management team, invested heavily in learning about models of cooperation. They traveled extensively in the United States and in Europe to study the best co-ops of the era.

What is unique about CSI is that as it's grown it has invested even heavier in the co-op ethos. CSI greatly differs from some co-ops, which tend to become less interested in promoting their cooperative aspects as they get larger. The credo of CSI is:

1. Open voluntary membership to all CSI building residents.

2. Democratic control, following the "one member, one vote" philosophy.

3. Non-profit operation, with surplus funds either used to provide additional member services or put into reserves. No individual owns the co-op or profits financially from it.

4. Continuing education, with CSI providing all the training residents need to manage and operate their buildings.

Democracy is the foundation for all decision-making and the basis for the operating philosophy at CSI. To become a member, you invest a one-time, refundable fee of $100. From that moment on, you have one vote in CSI's business affairs. Residents from each floor of a CSI co-op building elect a representative to a building council, which meets monthly and has authority over the budget process and local management. There also are a number of resident committees, such as membership, finance, recreation, decor and fund-raising.

The floor representatives report back to floor meetings to brief the members on the key actions. All building residents meet once a month in a general membership assembly to vote on specified council decisions and make recommendations to the council. Except for certain executive sessions discussing personnel, legal matters or real estate purchases, meetings on every element of the co-op's governance are open to all members.

The residents of each building also elect representatives to the National Cooperative Congress. At the congress, the building representatives nominate resident candidates for CSI's corporate board of directors. All CSI members then vote annually to elect the board from among the nominated members.

The national CSI board meets monthly to set policy and review management performance. It also approves annual building budgets and major building contracts. The congress reviews corporate issues with the board three times a year and maintains the linkage between the board and the co-op's general membership. Through these mechanisms, the congress ensures that CSI continues to be responsive to its members. Member residents are well-informed through regular newsletters produced by the residents themselves. Their newest tool will be an e-mail system that will allow every member in every building to communicate with CSI staff and fellow members – a project members are eagerly awaiting.

When opening CSI's 80-unit Roslingdale building, Boston Mayor Thomas Menino spoke about the importance of allowing tenants a voice in matters affecting them. CSI's commitment to participation was the major reason for his support of the project. "This is the type of housing we need all over the city," said Menino. At another opening of a CSI project, CSI's president and general manager Fred Wood said, "The purpose of the cooperative is for each member to have a say in how the apartments are run. The residents of the cooperative do this through the various elected committees. The people on the committees are the backbone of the cooperative. They do this on a strictly volunteer basis."

CSI's operating philosophy of encouraging a thriving democracy among the residents is in direct contrast to much of what happens in retirement communities in the United States. Compare CSI to the senior housing project called Hillhaven, featured in the PBS television program, "Waiting for God," imported from England. In this comedy a wily, cost-cutting housing manager focused on profits is always trying to get rid of an activist senior who spends her time standing up for residents' rights. While viewed as an infernal nuisance at Hillhaven, the heroine would be seen as a tremendous asset at CSI.

For most residents of a CSI building, life is centered around independent living. Most units are one-bedroom with a bathroom and kitchenette. The one-bedrooms prove to be the most popular. The units are equipped with a security call system to alert the office of any emergencies. CSI uses a number of government programs, which helps keep rent below the market rate and within reach of the low-income residents. All of the buildings also offer a number of units designed to be handicapped-accessible. Each building usually has a library, a community meeting room, an activities room, a laundry, a dining room and a kitchen facility. Although people love their own units, a favorite spot to meet is the dining room. Volunteers cook weekday meals for a small donation. Each building has a van to provide local transportation service.

CSI finances its development in numerous ways. For much of its history, CSI was a major customer of HUD's 202 program. With government cutbacks, CSI has branched out to use other financing sources, such as the tax credit program at the state level and housing bonds at the local level.

CSI's Fred Wood sees the organization focusing on its four-state area in the near term, with particular emphasis on opportunities in southern California. The reduction in federal government funding for all forms of housing makes for a more competitive marketplace with more groups chasing fewer resources. Wood also sees changes in the responses of communities to senior housing. "Because of funds, site availability and neighborhood response," Wood says, "communities are more favorable to projects from 40 to fewer than 100 units. It's interesting to note that the residents of the smaller buildings are proud of the fact that they know each other, while the residents in the larger building see the advantages of so many more volunteers for activities. For a number of cost and design reasons, three-story buildings are now more prevalent than high rises. The 100-plus unit projects so popular in the 1970s are much more difficult to get approved."

"Our co-op approach is great for seniors," adds Wood. "Because of our no-equity policy, our seniors are not looking for a return on investment but a return on their lifestyle. Their membership gains them social equity, and the units stay affordable forever. There is a great belief among CSI members that they are leaving something wonderful for the people who will follow them. They know the feeling well because they are all benefiting from the gift left by others."

FARMS, FAMILIES AND FRIENDS

There's probably no better place to plant seeds of cooperation than in the fertile soil of rural Minnesota. There in farm country, deep in the heart and rich heritage of populist America, good ideas and co-ops have a history of being made for each other. Today, a new wave of co-ops is sweeping across Minnesota and beyond to Wisconsin, Iowa and North and South Dakota. The new phenomenon, named Homestead Housing Center, has an enthusiastic base: the seniors of rural America. These small senior-housing co-ops (ranging from 16- to 30-unit complexes) are keeping families together in the small rural communities of the Upper Midwest.

Before Homestead Housing Co-op came to town, usually the only choice for middle-income rural people looking for senior housing was to move to a major city. Retirement meant moving hundreds of miles away from their farms, families and friends. In addition, each retiree who left home also left his or her rural community. "When they leave," points out Vaughan Sinclair, organizer of the first Homestead Co-op in St. James, MN, "they take their bank accounts, their shopping lists, their church donations and their leadership with them."

If they stay and form a cooperative, they pump much-needed activity into the local economy. For instance, the 26,000-square-foot building for the 16-unit Homestead Co-op in Hull, Iowa, required about 70 subcontractors overall. Local businesses did 70 percent of the subcontracting.

The Homestead co-ops also free up rural housing for families. The children can take over the family farm, or a young family can buy the house in town. When the Homestead co-op opened in Hull, for example, there were only seven homes for sale in the community of 1,900 people. The co-op created 16 new housing opportunities in the community. The 26-unit Homestead Co-op in Grand Marais, MN, had the same effect. "It's going to be a real plus for our community," says Grand Marais Mayor Andrea Peterson. "For a while it was really difficult to buy a house in town. When people move into cooperative housing, that frees up a lot of houses." Another advantage is that, unlike the non-profit, tax-exempt, subsidized units for low-income citizens, the co-op's units pay their fair share of a community's taxes.

The Homestead co-ops' occupants are too young and active to be in nursing homes. However, they appreciate not having to keep up their houses anymore. Often they state that they couldn't have withstood the loneliness of one more winter on the farm or the mowing of one more lawn.

Homestead Housing co-ops deal with one other major problem of senior housing in small-town America, most of which is for low-income seniors. Few facilities exist for moderate-income seniors, and of those that do, almost all are rental.

Thus, for many reasons, resources need to be available to rural America to halt the continuing outmigration of seniors to urban areas. The Homestead model is showing how this can be done.

To trace the beginnings of Homestead co-ops, we need to go back to the 1970s and '80s, when developers created a number of senior co-op housing units in rural and urban Minnesota. In particular, the Twin Cities of Minneapolis/St. Paul fostered many types of housing cooperatives; many of the most outstanding of these projects were for senior residents.

The differences between 7500 York Cooperative, a 338-unit senior housing co-op in Edina, MN, and a nearby large condominium for seniors had an effect upon Terry McKinley, a long-time mortgage lender for multifamily housing. The co-op always had a busy lobby, events were frequently taking place, and the residents were visibly more active. The condo lobby was generally empty, and there were few activities. From the day he first noticed the contrasts, the image of York Co-op's active seniors stayed with McKinley.

The sponsor of the 7500 York Cooperative was the Lutheran Church's Ebenezer Society in Minnesota. Testifying before the President's Commission on Housing in 1981, Gerry Glazer, a gerontologist working at the Ebenezer Society, remarked, "Resident control and self-determination are the major keys to the project's success. From a gerontological point of view, the essential benefit of the cooperative is that it provides an economic structure and social framework that fosters self-reliance, self-control and determination, interdependence and cooperation among the resident members, even among those with severe chronic conditions. As gerontologists, we know that these factors contribute directly to continued independent living, successful aging and the enhancement of longer life."

In the 1980s, McKinley began to work with a couple who were quietly putting together senior housing co-ops in small-town Minnesota. Their Realife Cooperative models were very popular, even though they were essentially developing them one project at a time. Once again McKinley noted the immediate enthusiasm seniors had for the co-op model. As he and other co-op housing leaders talked, they had to come to terms with the fact that the need in rural Minnesota far outstripped the capacity of the developer community. Solving the problem meant bridging the gap.

Fortunately, the Cooperative Development Foundation (CDF) noticed the extent of the senior housing opportunity in rural America. Based in Washington D.C., CDF was actively supporting the development of senior housing co-ops through its Kaplan Fund, which was endowed by Jacob M. Kaplan, a co-op entrepreneur who organized the farmers' co-op that markets Welch's grape juice. For much of his later life, Kaplan's philanthropic interests funded the development of housing co-ops for students and seniors. When he was in his 90s, he became the oldest living person inducted into the Cooperative Hall of Fame. Kaplan's vision was that cooperatives had a great deal to offer seniors, and seed money could support experiments and develop models. Although it has existed only a decade, the Kaplan Fund has had measurable impact across the United States.

In 1988, CDF combined predevelopment funds from the Kaplan Fund and the National Cooperative Bank Development Fund to support projects in southern Minnesota. CDF brought McKinley in to create the new organizational model. His insight into senior co-op housing in Minnesota and his commitment to creating a replicable model gave the new entity both its vision and its competence. Incorporated in 1991, Homestead Housing Center (HHC) emerged to carry the co-op flag into the rural communities. McKinley is now president of HHC, and he's probably seen more of the Midwest than most U.S. presidential candidates.

One by one the characteristics that shaped HHC began to form. The first was that there needed to be a local board of directors willing to raise local predevelopment money, market the co-op, work with the local authorities and give credence to the project. The smartest initial idea was inviting diverse co-op organizations to become sponsors of the local effort. As a result, each Homestead project gains immediate board capacity, local trust and respect.

Homestead's first co-op project broke ground in St. James, MN, in 1993. Vaughan Sinclair, the retired manager of a local co-op grain elevator, took the lead. With his irrepressible sense of humor and optimism, Sinclair is a great people-person and knows how to manage projects. At the time, he served on the board of directors of Nationwide Insurance Enterprises. Sinclair's stature in the community meant that when he talked, people listened. Now Homestead was ready to spring into action. One by one the sponsors came on: St. Paul Bank for Cooperatives, Agribank, Farm Credit of St. Paul, Cenex, Land O'Lakes, United Power Association (jointly owned by electric cooperatives) and Wausau Insurance Companies (a Wisconsin-based insurer owned by Nationwide Enterprises), as well as CDF. The local group headed by Sinclair raised $25,000. With matching funds from the Homestead consortium, development of the St. James project began.

The St. James Homestead Cooperative is a one-level building of 23 units of excellent housing in what was until recently a cornfield. The opening prices ranged from $49,700 for a one-bedroom apartment to $86,700 for a two-bedroom, two-bath apartment. Each unit has its own indoor garage. All areas are barrier-free and senior-friendly to encourage independent living. Additional on-site facilities include a social room, exercise room, a guest room for visitors, a workshop and a laundry room. The co-op's living units have emergency response systems, and there is a centralized security access for visitors and guests. Each Homestead also provides a garden area for residents to practice their fine-tuned skills. There's an on-site manager, and each co-op has a minivan to provide local transportation. Residents pay from $160 to $280 monthly for property taxes, insurance, maintenance and transportation service. This fee includes everything except for individual telephone and utility costs.

In St. James and most of the other Homestead co-ops, the residents generally purchase their units outright with money from the sale of their farms or former homes. Many of the co-ops have few outstanding loans and only limited interest costs. The Homestead co-ops have all of the same characteristics as home ownership. Therefore, interest and real estate taxes are deductible from each owner's federal and state taxes. When members leave, their units are sold to people on a waiting list. Members are guaranteed that upon sale they will receive their initial cost plus 1 percent per year.

Each of the Homestead co-ops is independent and owned outright by the local resident members or their families. Eligible occupants must be 55 and older. Each unit has one vote in the election of the board and the co-op's affairs. The board acts in all matters on behalf of the members, such as approving the various contracts for maintenance, upkeep and repairs of the co-op, plus other services approved by members.

Speaking at the groundbreaking ceremonies at St. James, John Gauci, executive director of CDF said, "Eventually we're looking for a nationwide system for seniors to run their lives as they see fit. This is something needed in this country: seniors living independently while staying active in the communities where they have their roots." Others began to see the potential. In 1993, the Joel L. Parkin Fund granted money to CDF to fund the further development of Midwest senior housing co-ops.

Who moves into the Homestead Housing co-ops? A survey of three of the co-ops revealed some interesting facts. Of the residents, 95 percent were retired, while 56 percent had no disability and 34 percent had some form of disability (with 10 percent not responding to that question). In terms of annual income, 23 percent earned less than $10,000, 33 percent earned $10,001 to $20,000, and another 23 percent earned from $20,001 to $40,000. The marital status was 2 percent single, 36 percent married and 62 percent widowed. Ages ranged from 62 to 91, with the median age at 80. On the basis of gender, 23 percent were male and 77 percent were female.

Before moving to the co-op, 95 percent had owned their own home, 38 percent had lived in a rural area, and 54 percent had lived in a town with a population of 10,000 or less. The mean distance from their previous home was nine miles, with two miles being the median distance. The residents had lived in their previous homes for an average of 31 years. Seventy-two percent of them had previously lived alone, for an average period of 13 years.

The three most important reasons that influenced their decision to move to the co-op were: (1) Wanting a home that I could take care of easily (89 percent); (2) Wanting a home where I have a say in how it's run (76 percent); and (3) Wanting to stay in my own home community (74 percent).

The three major benefits of the co-op cited by residents were: (1) It provides me with a community of friends (91 percent); (2) It gives me a voice in how my housing is run (85%); and (3) It provides opportunities to work with others on common goals (84 percent). When asked about the effect of co-op living, the top three answers were: ease of maintaining my home (97 percent), personal safety (95 percent) and life satisfaction (92 percent).

Today, the Homestead Housing Center assists leadership groups in communities to develop cooperative housing for middle-income seniors. HHC provides analysis of community needs; arranges for seed capital and project financing; organizes the local leadership and forms the cooperative corporation; coordinates marketing, architectural design and construction; and, finally, provides assistance to the local co-op's management through the first year.

By the end of 1995, HHC had established 16 Homestead Housing co-ops in the previous three years. One of the latest to emerge is the 26-unit project in Grand Marais, MN. For the previous 10 years, a group in Grand Marais had been trying to build middle- income senior housing in their community. With the help of HHC, their dream finally moved to the drawing board.

From a policy perspective, America needs to address the issue of the rural elderly. Of people age 65 and over, 75 percent to 85 percent are homeowners. They have substantial equity tied up in their homes and are seriously considering other housing options. Important to them is continued control over their housing, continued tax benefits and equity growth they can pass on to their heirs. They wish to remain in their communities, yet they want more security, especially as related to health concerns. They worry about having to travel 40 miles to the nearest hospital in a medical emergency, such as a heart attack.

HHC believes that cooperatives are a proven form of ownership. They cost less to construct and operate, and they have the lowest form of default rate of any housing option. Unlike some of the other ownership options that require large endowments, co-ops such as Homestead require only a $500 reservation deposit. The purchase of the unit is like that of the home. When you leave the co-op, you sell at the market price, and the sale proceeds are yours. There are no hidden gimmicks, no fine print, no additional contracts. You choose when to buy your unit and when to sell. The residents control their costs through their elected board and adoption of the annual budget. The minutes are posted and a board member probably lives one door down the hall, or it could easily be you.

In 1996, HHC expanded again into Kansas, Missouri and Nebraska. The added sponsors in the new region are CoBank ACB (Denver),

Farmland Industries, Inc. (Kansas City, MO), the Kansas Cooperative Council (Topeka, KS) and NW Electric Power Cooperative (Cameron, MO).

Dennis Johnson, president of St. Paul Bank for Cooperatives and HHC chair, explains, "Our purpose is to help rural communities provide unsubsidized housing alternatives for middle-income seniors. These cooperatives provide facilities and basic services for independent seniors, in an environment they own and control. In the process, it frees up single-family homes for younger families."

He adds, "As more Homestead cooperatives have been completed, and word has spread, we have received many requests from other states. We are delighted that regional cooperatives there have gotten behind the expansion, as we have found this type of local leadership to be crucial to success of these new housing cooperatives."

The future for Homestead is one of great challenge. The need is evident, and the requests for help are more than can be handled. Clearly the cooperative model has great potential to provide a future for senior citizens in the communities where they have spent most of their lives and where their families live. The ability to remain independent and to live an active life is the gift given by the Homestead model.

NORC: A NEW ACRONYM FOR A NEW SITUATION

The 1980s were a decade of increasing problems for the once proud Penn South housing co-op in New York City. The problems had started slowly, but incidents kept on increasing. Each week, stories circulated of residents who were not paying their rent, not turning off faucets or gas, not cashing Social Security checks, not hearing from their neighbors for a week, and found wandering around the halls. Then the incident occurred that touched everyone the most: A naked elderly woman had climbed the stairs onto the roof, could not find her way back and had frozen to death. What was the cause of these events and what could be done?

The answer lay in the origins of the co-op located at 8th Avenue from 23rd to 29th Streets. Built in the early 1960s, Penn South's 2,820 units of co-op housing were sponsored by the International Ladies Garment Workers Union (ILGWU). The co-op created new homes in the heart of New York City – homes for the working men and women who were union members, and who had young families in a city of few opportunities. This was their one chance at home ownership.

These people were in the crowd when an American president spoke at the opening of the co-op. In an historic dedication on May 19, 1962, President John F. Kennedy said prophetically, "It is the task of every generation to build a road for the next generation. This housing development can provide a better life for the people who come after us, if we meet our responsibilities."

By the 1980s, the co-op's demographics had changed dramatically. The young families had disappeared. The kids had grown up and left home. Apartment by apartment, Penn South's population had aged in place. By 1994, more than 5,000 of Penn South's 6,200 residents (80 percent) were over age 62, and the average age was 76. Penn South had become the city's largest naturally occurring retirement community, or NORC, as they're referred to today. And that was the reason for all the problems. The young people who had started the co-op had mostly never left, and now they were suffering all the symptoms that go with aging.

What was unique was not how Penn South discovered the problem, but how it went about solving it. In 1986, board president David Smith met with social service experts from the United Jewish Appeal - Federation (UJA-F) to discuss how to deal with the rising social and health concerns occurring at the co-op. The first step was the creation of the Penn South Program for Seniors (PSPS), a consortium of Self-help Community Services and the Jewish Home and Hospital for the Aged. Today, many observers view the PSPS program as the leading one of its kind in the United States.

When you enter the PSPS facility, you grasp immediately how the program is a rich quilt made up of opportunities taken. The 3,200-square-foot first floor was once Penn South's storage room. Fortunately, the facility is separated from the remainder of the 10-building housing complex. which allows it to be quieter, independent and to have its own image.

The building is now a busy maze of offices and cubicles that offer a one-stop social service center providing case management, counseling, medical assistance, an emergency response system and recreational activities. The center arranges for companion visits, medical care, home attendants, food delivery and other services to keep people functioning independently in their homes. The program offers classes, lectures and workshops. The center is almost always busy from 9 a.m. to 5 p.m. Membership in the center costs $15 annually, with scholarships available to those who cannot afford the fee. PSPS now has more than 700 members.

The center has a paid staff of about a dozen people. A frequent compliment to the program is that it integrates the social program with the social and health services. The center couldn't operate, however, were it not for the hundreds of volunteers who donate time to the program. They help deliver the program, raise money and teach classes. Each of the 10- week semesters offers about 20 classes, half of them taught by volunteers. Yiddish courses often attract nearly 50 residents. In particular, the cultural events bring a special joy to those members who can't get to the theater as they used to. The program now serves more than 1,000 people, including 300 frail and homebound residents whose average age is 85.

The PSPS program has an annual budget of about $400,000 and receives about $120,000 from UJA-F. Penn South's board contributes $100,000 from its operating budget to the center. The remainder comes from the State Office of Aging (under new NORC legislation which Penn South helped develop), the City's Department of Aging and a number of foundations. The co-op's members help out, too. Some voluntarily check off on their rent a sum of $10 or $15 a month to go to the center. Members also are encouraged to sign over the equity in their unit to the center as a bequest to the program.

One of the dynamos behind PSPS' success is David Smith, who at 77 years young qualified for the program many years ago. Now president emeritus of Penn South, Smith is a renowned fund raiser whose charm and persistence are legendary. It was only recently that Smith ran his last marathon. He serves on the board of the National Cooperative Business Association and raises the most money of any individual each year for the "Race for Cooperative Development." Since helping set up PSPS, he's now involved in developing a city-wide program of support for NORCs.

Beginning with Penn South, the NORC program has spread to other co-op complexes in New York City, including Warbasse Houses in Coney Island and Co-op Village on the Lower East Side. The UJA-F put together a consortium of agencies providing transportation, legal and other counseling, regular health checkups, case management and access to area hospitals.

Recognizing the work being done by the NORCs, the UJA and other co-ops worked to win passage of state legislation that appropriated $1 million in 1994 to match such efforts in ten NORCs. This is the first state funding made available to NORCs in the United States.

The need continues to grow. Most importantly, the NORC model comes along at a time when policy planners from the different disciplines of housing, health care and social services are looking for alternatives to nursing homes or hospitalization for senior citizens. It's not only the cost of those options to the state, but also the emotional and financial devastation to the patients that keeps everyone looking for other options. Keeping people in their own homes and communities is better medicine for body and soul.

It's estimated that 27 percent of all older Americans live in NORCs. In New York City alone, about 250,000 people live in government-assisted NORCs. In a city of 1.27 million elderly, with 15 percent of those below the poverty line, senior housing is hard to find. Places like Penn South give a great deal of comfort and security to its members.

For people like Penn South resident Sara Liebowitz, age 91, PSPS was like gaining a new friend. Her doctor told her she'd have to start taking insulin for her diabetes. How could she give herself the needle? In fear, she called PSPS for assistance. The center sent a registered nurse who taught Liebowitz how to use the needle and came every day until she was sure she was doing it right. The nurse still visits once a week to check Liebowitz's blood sugar and see how she's doing.

In another situation, a man with Parkinson's disease was getting by but needed home-care services. One Friday, the center got a call from Meals on Wheels saying they couldn't get into his apartment. The center sent over a nurse who, after conferring with the man's doctor, realized that a change in his medication was the cause of the problem. If the center hadn't been on site, an outside social worker would have been called, and the man would have been taken to the hospital for the weekend until his doctor could see him. In this instance, the nurse was able to show the man that he needed to have home-care visits. He now gets visits regularly and feels secure.

PSPS is a pioneer model that's finding solutions to new problems. Its leadership has initiated innovation in program delivery. As a result, the seniors living at Penn South have increasing confidence in a support system that's as near as the telephone and just around the corner. NORCs are on the increase all around the United States. Those looking for answers to similar problems need to visit the Penn South Program. You'll know you're in the right place when you walk into the former first floor storage room. The attitudes and activities of the people in the room tell you that in this corner of New York City, they have found success.

CONCLUSION

There is no one-size-fits-all approach to senior housing, as evidenced by the examples detailed in this chapter. Seniors are as diverse a collection of individuals as any other age group. Thus, their housing needs also span across the spectrum. Some, for instance, can live completely independently; others need various degrees of health care and other assistance in order to live comfortably.

While the co-op housing solutions described in this chapter are diverse, there are some elements in common:

1. Resident control and active involvement - These projects are not examples of someone "doing for" seniors, but rather "doing with" them. Co-ops allow seniors a voice in setting policies, pricing decisions and managing their housing. Governance is in their hands.

2. Building coalitions - Projects can get off to a faster, more successful start by building working alliances with local governments, other cooperatives, community organizations and businesses.

3. Aging in place - No one likes to be abruptly uprooted. Seniors are no different. Successful housing co-ops give seniors the opportunity to stay in the community where they have lived most of their lives. Thus, for rural and urban seniors alike, there's no need to move to some senior facility on the other side of the city or county.

4. Vibrant living communities - Housing co-ops such as the ones in this chapter are much more than just roofs over seniors' heads. They are active centers that enhance seniors' opportunities for continued fruitful living, learning and socializing.

ACKNOWLEDGMENTS
Noreen Beiro, Vice President, National Cooperative Bank Development Corporation, San Francisco, CA

Herb Brown, Secretary, Leisureville Community Assoc., Woodland, CA

Julie Fox, Administrative Assistant, Homestead Housing Center, Inver Grove Heights, MN

John Gauci, Coordinator, CLUSA Institute, Washington, D.C.

Terry McKinley, President, Homestead Housing Center, Inver Grove Heights, MN

David Smith, Chairman of the Board, Penn South, New York City, NY

Virginia and Fred Thornthwaite, Founders, Cooperative Services Inc.(CSI), Oak Park, MI

Jerry and Chris Rioux, HCD Services, Grass Valley, CA

Karen Strauss, Executive Director, Penn South Program for Seniors, New York, NY

Donald Wells, President, Leisureville Community Assoc., Woodland, CA

Fred Wood, General Manager, Cooperative Services Inc. (CSI), Oak Park, MI

REFERENCES AND SOURCES
Smith, David and Vladeck, Fredda. 1990. "The Cooperative Movement Creates an Innovative Response Integrating Senior Services and Housing." *Cooperative Housing Bulletin.* September/October: 8-18

Thompson, David J. 1996. "Renters Fight Back and Find Their Freedom." *Cooperative Housing Bulletin.* May/June: 10-12.

CHAPTER 7.

THE CONSUMER MOVEMENT AMONG PEOPLE WITH DISABILITIES

People with disabilities are the largest minority group in the United States. In the past several decades they have also become powerful and effective advocates for their own civil and consumer rights. In all parts of the United States from the late 1960s to the mid-1990s, people with disabilities and their allies formed hundreds of locally based, consumer-governed "independent living centers" to help people with physical and mental impairments have access to basic rights and services in their communities – accessible housing, transportation, jobs and other ordinary needs most nondisabled people take for granted.

Although not formal cooperatives, independent living centers are models of cooperation. Most of the board members – the people who make policy decisions – at each center are people with disabilities. Most staff members have disabilities. The overriding goal of each center is to help the disabled consumers it serves overcome the obstacles that the nondisabled world puts in their way and attain as much control over their lives as possible. Cooperative action is thus the cornerstone of the independent living movement. This chapter presents information on the origins and development of this movement and provides examples of centers in California, Maine, Montana and Wisconsin.

Ed Roberts, Independent Living Advocate, 1939-1995

Ed Roberts died in March 1995, while the first draft of this chapter was being written. He was unknown to most of us, but to people with disabilities around the world, he is known as the father of the independent living movement. His commitment, energy and creativity in support of the rights of people with disabilities will be greatly missed.

When Roberts was 14, he contracted polio. As a result, he became a quadriplegic who relied on a respirator during the day and an iron lung at night throughout his life. Shortly after his polio attack, he overheard the family doctor tell his mother that he would never be more than a vegetable. As an adult, he joked that if he was going to be a vegetable, he wanted to be an artichoke, "prickly on the outside with a tender heart."

Roberts did anything but vegetate. He graduated from high school despite the fact that the principal wanted to withhold his diploma because he didn't pass his driver's education class. He and his mother overcame this obstacle by convincing the school board to overrule the principal. Roberts did very well as a student at the local community college, and his application was accepted at the University of California at Berkeley. But his disabilities were not. As the dean of students put it, "We've tried cripples and it didn't work." He won this one, too, entering Berkeley in 1962 as the school's first student with severe disabilities. James Meredith broke the color barrier at the University of Mississippi that same semester. "We both had to sue to get into school," Roberts reflected years later. He completed his master's degree in political science while at Berkeley.

Roberts' extracurricular activities overshadowed his scholarly accomplishments. He and a small group of other quadriplegics who joined him at Berkeley began what later came to be called the independent living movement. The group, known as the Rolling Quads, received funding in 1970 for a Physically Disabled Students' Program. The philosophy of this program emphatically rejected the "doctor knows best" approach. "People with disabilities," said the Berkeley group, "were consumers, not patients. Like consumers, they needed to select rather than settle."

When the program office was inundated with requests for assistance from nonstudents, it quickly became apparent that similar services were needed by the disabled citizens of Berkeley as well as on campus. In 1972, the Center for Independent Living was established to address this need, with Ed Roberts as its first executive director.

In 1975, Roberts was appointed the director of California's Department of Rehabilitation, the same department that initially had refused to sponsor his college education on the grounds that he was "too disabled to work." In his new job, he immediately provided funding for nine additional Centers for Independent Living (CILs) based on the Berkeley model. Joan Leon, the executive vice president of the World Institute on Disability, reflected on Roberts' leadership at the Department of Rehabilitation: "I don't think you could have sold the concept of independent living on the basis of one CIL. But by [showing that the concept worked in 10 centers] he started something that was absolutely unstoppable."

Roberts went on to co-found with Judy Heumann the World Institute on Disability, where he continued his efforts to expand the independent living movement in the United States and internationally until his death in 1995. As Marca Bristo, president of Access Living in Chicago, said after Roberts' death: "He was one of a kind ... He believed in himself before others did, and found power inside of himself, and then shared that power with millions and millions of people. He made us believe in ourselves."

OUT OF SIGHT, OUT OF MIND

When most of us in the United States are asked about civil rights, the first thing that comes to mind is African-Americans in the 1960s – Martin Luther King, Jr., the Montgomery bus boycott, and related images of Black Americans seeking equal treatment in education, jobs, housing and other areas in which they had faced a long history of discrimination. Many of us also think about the civil rights movements among women, American Indians, Hispanic Americans, other racial and ethnic groups, and gay people.

Few of us, however, consider the efforts of people with disabilities over the past 25 years to assert their rights to equal access in our society. You might be surprised to learn that people with disabilities constitute the largest minority group in the United States with an estimated 49 million members, according to a 1994 U.S. census report. It's also the only minority group that any of us may join at any time either through injury or illness. The civil rights movement among disabled people has grown in size, visibility and power since the first independent living center was established in Berkeley in 1972. But it's still largely invisible.

Or, is it? How many curbs have you seen lately that are not ramped for wheelchairs? How many office buildings and stores can you think of that don't have handicapped parking or handicapped-accessible entrances? How many of you have workmates or people with whom you interact on a day-to-day basis who have disabilities? Just 10 years ago your answers to these questions would have been very different.

The purpose of this chapter is to take a look at the opening up of American society to people with disabilities. During the past quarter of a century, there has been a major shift in American politics and in American culture away from underestimating the abilities of disabled people and away from warehousing them in nursing homes and other institutions. In recent years there has been significant movement at the federal, state and local levels and in the private sector toward the removal of barriers that block the access of people with physical and mental impairments to education, jobs and independent housing. These changes didn't just happen. They were the result of a long, difficult struggle successfully waged by people with disabilities and their families and friends. This struggle was, and continues to be, both a civil rights movement (changing and enforcing laws) and a consumer movement (gaining access to essential goods and services and having a voice in how they are provided).

In order for this story to make sense, however, some definitions are in order. A person with a disability is anyone who has a physical or mental impairment that limits his or her ability to perform certain activities. Disabilities can be moderate, such as Senator Bob Dole's partially paralyzed arm or Neil Bush's learning disability, or they can be severe, as in the case of some people with quadriplegia who may have little or no use of their arms and legs. Some of the most common kinds of disabilities are mobility impairments caused by spinal cord injuries, amputations, neuromuscular disease and cerebral palsy; visual impairments; hearing impairments; mental retardation; mental illness; and traumatic brain injury.

The word "consumer" has a special significance as used in this chapter. Historically, people with disabilities have been viewed as patients or clients by the individuals and institutions that "took care of them." As consumers, disabled people make their own choices about how they live, the services they receive and from whom they receive these services. For people who have had extremely limited choices about their lives in the past, becoming a consumer is a liberating experience. This definition of consumer is consistent with the one used by the cooperative movement. A consumer cooperative is a business that is owned and controlled by the people who purchase goods and services from it. Thus, in a consumer cooperative, the consumer is ultimately in charge.

There are a number of consumer cooperatives in which people with disabilities are active members. Elderly and disabled housing co-ops, such as those developed by Cooperative Services, Inc. based in Michigan and Homestead Housing Center based in Minnesota (see chapter 6), feature barrier-free design. Mariposa Villa in Irvine, CA, is a co-op designed for people with disabilities. ADOBES, Inc. in Massachusetts and Co-op Initiatives in Connecticut are both non-profit associations that develop co-op housing for people with and without disabilities. There are also food co-ops, buying clubs, cooperative preschools, health co-ops, transportation co-ops, personal service co-ops, dining co-ops, credit unions, and purchasing and repair co-ops for wheelchairs and other equipment – all designed to meet the needs of people with disabilities. Deborah Altus' **Consumer Co-ops: A Resource Guide for Consumers with Disabilities** is an excellent source of information on these co-ops.

While the consumer movement among people with disabilities and the consumer cooperative movement have many things in common, it is important to note that centers for independent living and many other organizations controlled by people with disabilities are non-profit service organizations. Although not formal cooperatives, they espouse cooperative values because people with disabilities – the consumers – play an active role in governing and staffing the centers and because services are provided in a consumer-responsive manner.

THE INDEPENDENT LIVING MOVEMENT

"For those of us who have disabilities, being in a nursing home is like being imprisoned for a crime we didn't commit," said Bob Deist, assistant director of Personal Care at Access to Independence in Madison, WI, in an interview for this chapter.

It's impossible to understand the history of the consumer movement among disabled people without first understanding the medical philosophy regarding the disabled that pervaded the United States well into the 1980s and still persists in the minds of some health-care professionals and policy-makers today. During most of the 20th century, people with severe disabilities were to be kept at home or in institutions and out of the public eye. The general belief was that people with severe disabilities could not lead useful lives. Therefore, access to education and to jobs was not even a consideration. In his excellent book, **No Pity: People with Disabilities Forging a New Civil Rights Movement**, Joseph Shapiro chronicles the dramatic shift away from this medical model and toward independent living. The opening of the Center for Independent Living in Berkeley in 1972 is often cited as the symbol of this shift in philosophy.

By 1977, there were an estimated 52 centers around the United States. Within the next 10 years the number of centers mushroomed to about 300. Today about 400 centers are in operation. Approximately two-thirds of these centers subscribe to the four major provisions of the Independent Living Center Charter:

1. The majority of the board of directors are people with disabilities.

2. Services are provided to people with a range of different disabilities.

3. At least the following four core services are provided: peer counseling; independent living skills training; information and referral; and advocacy.

4. All services are consumer-driven.

The spread of these independent living centers represents an amazing grass-roots consumer movement. In a period of just 15 years, the United States went from having virtually no consumer-responsive services for disabled people to a national network of such services controlled by disabled people.

There is a political side to this story as well. During the Nixon administration, a civil rights provision was included in the Rehabilitation Act of 1973.

No otherwise qualified handicapped individual in the United States shall, solely by reason of his handicap, be excluded from the participation in, be denied the benefits of, or be subject to discrimination under any program or activity receiving federal financial assistance. (Section 504)

No clear historical record exists of just how this language ended up in the act, but it was to have profound repercussions on the entire society. Draft regulations for this handicapped civil rights provision were prepared, but not completed, during the Ford administration. Recognizing the far-reaching economic and political impact of this simple paragraph, Joseph Califano, the Secretary of Health, Education and Welfare under Jimmy Carter, tried to water it down with a set of revised regulations. But a series of sit-ins by people with disabilities and their allies in Washington, D.C., San Francisco and in other cities, as well as a strong public reaction, convinced the administration to leave it alone. Four years and two presidents after the Rehabilitation Act was signed into law by President Nixon, Califano signed the final regulations implementing the handicapped civil rights provision. Among many other things, Section 504 was the beginning of national requirements for access by the disabled to sidewalks, parking places, public transportation and public buildings – conditions we now take for granted.

A year later another federal policy breakthrough occurred when, after listening to testimony from Ed Roberts and other disability rights advocates, Congress gave Rehabilitation Services the discretion to provide funding for CILs. The availability of federal financial assistance was a key factor in the six-fold increase in the number of centers during the next decade.

The next major political steps toward increasing the rights of people with disabilities occurred during the Reagan and Bush administrations. The Americans with Disabilities Act was signed into law in 1990 by President Bush and took effect in 1992. It's an equal rights, not an "equal results" – or affirmative action – law. It provides basic civil rights for people with disabilities – the right to see a movie, go shopping, buy a house, apply for a job – without being denied access because of a disability. One of the reasons that this far-reaching law developed and eventually passed during two conservative administrations is the fact that disabilities extend across all class, political, color and gender lines. Both Republicans and Democrats were persuaded by the argument that having a disability should not be an excuse to deny someone an opportunity to participate in society – especially when the argument was being presented forcefully and effectively by the very people who were being denied these basic rights.

The rest of this chapter presents four examples of centers for independent living: an update on the very first CIL in Berkeley; a look at a center in Maine that created a for-profit subsidiary to sell and repair equipment for the disabled; a center in Montana that is grappling with the problems of providing consumer services in dispersed rural communities; and Access to Independence in Wisconsin, which is heavily involved in the provision of home-care services and in a pioneering project to establish a statewide health-care network controlled by the state's CILs.

DIVERSIFICATION IN BERKELEY

The Berkeley Center for Independent Living is the national and international prototype for a revolutionary organizational model governed and staffed by people with disabilities. Its own path through the last two decades, however, has not been an easy one. In some ways, Berkeley has mirrored the ups and downs experienced throughout the independent living movement during this time.

The center continued to expand its array of services and the number of people served after Ed Roberts left to become the director of the California Rehabilitation Agency in 1976. It was hit hard, however, by the cutbacks of the early Reagan years. At the beginning of 1980, the center operated 20 different programs at four sites. It had an operating budget of $3.2 million with more than 200 staff people. In 1981, the center lost more than $2 million in federal funds. By 1982, the budget was down to $735,000, and only 27 staff positions remained. Programs were slashed, and the number of people served had dropped by 50 percent.

Since that time, the Berkeley ILC has been able to build itself back up gradually. The major change the center made was to diversify its funding sources. During the first half of the 1990s, only half of the center's budget depended on government funds. All of its core services were privately funded. In 1995, the center's focus was on more efficient delivery of services through a combination of a staff reorganization; a continuation of diversified sources of funding, including fees generated from some services and publications; and a renewed level of advocacy opposing potential state and federal cutbacks.

ENTREPRENEURSHIP IN MAINE

Alpha One was established in 1979, the first year that funds were available under the National Rehabilitation Act to support centers for independent living. Right from the start, Alpha One's director Steve

Tremblay and his board had some unique ideas about the organization's mission. Tremblay, a wheelchair-user himself resulting from a spinal cord injury, came to Alpha One with a business background. He figured that the best way to provide for the long-term financial stability of the center was to run it like a business. Thus, Alpha One has a range of fee-based services, including consulting services to architects, lawyers and local governments on transportation, building access and other issues and to schools regarding their driver's education training programs.

But what really sets Alpha One apart from other CILs in the United States is its for-profit subsidiary, Wheelchairs Unlimited. This wholly owned company was established in 1986 to sell and service disability equipment and supplies. The company has stores in Portland and Augusta. Its eight employees operate a 24-hour equipment repair service, which is particularly valuable to people who use motorized wheelchairs. The company experienced small losses or just broke even during its first few years of operation, but has been profitable ever since. During the current fiscal year, the company will make a net profit of about $90,000 on around $900,000 in gross sales.

What's next for this entrepreneurial CIL? Alpha One is planning to form a health maintenance organization or a joint venture with an established HMO in order to make sure the future health-care needs of people with disabilities will be met in a consumer-responsive way. According to Tremblay, "Whether we like it or not, we are going to see more and more managed health-care systems. If Alpha One doesn't become actively involved, our consumers will suffer, because health-care providers generally don't understand the needs of people with disabilities." Alpha One's planned move into managed health care has another motive as well: further diversifying the financial base and, thus, the long-term economic stability of the organization.

BIG SKY AND BIG DISTANCES IN MONTANA

Summit Independent Living Center is headquartered in Missoula, MT, and has three satellite service centers in adjacent rural counties. Missoula itself has fewer than 40,000 inhabitants. As center director Mike Mayer puts it, "If you drive five miles in any direction from the center of Missoula, you're in the country." There are a total of 94,000 people in the counties served by the satellite centers. The biggest town outside Missoula has a population of 11,000. The sparse population makes for a lot of challenges in meeting the transportation, housing, personal attendant care and other needs of rural residents with disabilities. Since it began operation in 1981, Summit has developed effective, consumer-directed programs that have successfully overcome many of these challenges.

Summit started out as a federally funded project of the local rehabilitation center, which in turn was a part of Missoula's non-profit Community Medical Center. Summit maintained this status until 1988, when it became a freestanding independent living center governed by its own board of directors, a majority of whom have disabilities. Summit staff and its advisory committee had been advocating for autonomy for a number of years. But the medical center was reluctant to spin off the project. The impetus for the formal separation was a change in federal requirements, which made it a condition of federal funding that centers be governed by boards who had a majority of disabled members.

For its first four years, Summit served the Missoula area exclusively and restricted its services to wheelchair-users and others with mobility impairments. In 1985, it broadened its services to include the three adjacent counties and to provide assistance to people with other disabilities, such as visual and hearing impairments and multiple sclerosis. The center's level of activity in the three rural counties was limited – a total of two to three staff days per month in the three counties combined.

It wasn't until 1991 that Summit was able to make a major commitment to its rural constituents, thanks to the Robert Wood Johnson Foundation's one-year planning grant and three-year implementation grant, which provided the center with the resources necessary to establish comprehensive rural programs. In addition to the grant, the key to this rural initiative has been the primary role of local advisory councils in determining each county's priorities. These councils are comprised of a mix of disabled community residents, health-care professionals and local government officials. Each county now has its own staffed center providing peer counselor training, assistance in finding personal attendants and other services. In addition, Summit is helping these communities tackle difficult issues, such as transportation services for the mobility impaired and accessible housing, stores and offices.

The Robert Wood Johnson Foundation grant was completed in the fall of 1994. Summit is still readjusting to a smaller budget. The slack has been picked up in part by a United Way grant, in part through fee-for-service work (in particular, architectural consulting), but primarily through a reallocation of Summit's resources, some of which have been shifted from Missoula to the rural centers. To continue the staffing in the rural centers, there are three fewer program staff and two fewer administrative staff in the Missoula office. Mayer reports that "the current staffing level of nine employees and the budget of $330,000 is adequate for Summit's expanded service area. But it was a painful process to scale down operations after completion of the grant."

Summit faces several big issues now and for the coming years. One of these is compliance with the Americans with Disabilities Act. The center has found that just because a law is on the books doesn't mean it automatically gets enforced. Especially in rural communities, many local governments and businesses need a lot of nudging to install curb cuts, make buildings wheelchair-accessible, comply with housing code requirements and provide transportation services.

Through their statewide disability council, Summit and the other three centers for independent living in Montana have found some targeted nudging is required at the state level as well. For example, they achieved a big victory last year when they got the state Medicaid rules changed to remove the monopoly status that one personal-care vendor had for all Medicaid-funded attendants in the state. The rules were changed to allow consumers themselves to select and supervise their care providers.

Summit also shares a major concern with most other CILs. How will it maintain a stable budget in the face of potential federal and state cuts? Summit's answer for now is to run a lean organization and base its financing on a diversified strategy of public funding, local private support, limited fee-for-service income and selected private grants. As Mayer cautions, however: "We have learned not to go after just any grant. We want ones that are in keeping with our mission and priorities and that don't pull us in too many directions at the same time."

Fourteen years ago Summit started out as a small part of a much bigger organization that provided services to a fraction of the disabled community in one urban area. Now it's an independent, consumer-governed organization serving people with a wide range of disabilities in a four-county area. And it's having a statewide impact on improving the quality of life for people with disabilities. Summit also can serve as a national model of how to provide disability services to a combination of urban and rural areas in ways that are responsive to the needs of consumers in both types of communities.

ACCESSING INDEPENDENCE AND JOINT VENTURING IN WISCONSIN

At about the same time that the Center for Independent Living was established in Berkeley, a group of disabled people in Madison, WI, formed MOBIL (Madison Organization Behind Independent Living). Through most of the 1970s, this group advocated to make Madison a more accessible community. They succeeded in getting downtown curb cuts, transportation services, community housing and other improvements. When federal funding came along in 1978, they were ready with an application, and Access to Independence opened its doors the following year. The activists who comprised MOBIL continued to be the core of the Access board of directors in the 1980s.

Like many other centers, Access has experienced tremendous growth since its formation 16 years ago. Also, like these other centers, Access has tried to remain true to its initial goals and services. As Maureen Arcand, one of the founders of Access, wrote in 1994:

"The goal remains the same: To enable people to live in the community and make their own choices about where and how they want to live. The core services [also remain the same:] information and referral, peer support, housing counseling, and attendant care."

The founding mothers and fathers of Access would never have guessed what would become the major activity of the center in 1995 – the employment of some 200 personal-care workers. The historical role for CILs regarding personal-care attendants has been to help disabled consumers screen and select attendants. In keeping with the independent living philosophy, consumers have had the right to hire, supervise and fire their attendants. When Medicaid funds became available to pay for personal-care attendants in the early 1990s, there were bureaucratic strings attached. In particular, consumers whose attendants were paid for by Medicaid could not directly employ them. In order to continue to keep attendant-care services responsive to disabled consumers, Access decided to get directly into the attendant-care business. Thus, in May 1995, Access had a total of 230 employees, 200 of whom were full- and part-time attendant-care providers. Access continues to operate its attendant-care program in a consumer-responsive way. Consumers select their own attendants, supervise them and, if necessary, get attendants replaced. The difference is that under the Medicaid program, Access is the employer, not the disabled person receiving the service.

Even though the current system is working well for Access, the board and senior staff do not want to see the counseling and advocacy relationship with their consumers eroded by the administration of one large program. Accordingly, Access to Independence has been working closely with Eldercare, a non-profit organization serving the elderly, the Wisconsin Department of Health and Social Services and the Robert Wood Johnson Foundation on a plan to create a statewide network of non-profit disability and elderly organizations to provide comprehensive health-care services for their consumers. Access plans to separate its personal-care program into a non-profit subsidiary and to retain core counseling, training and advocacy services within the parent organization.

The effect of these changes will be similar to Alpha One's plans in Maine. A consortium of Wisconsin independent living centers and elderly-care providers will establish health maintenance organizations responsible for home-care services as well as broader medical services.

This program will allow disabled and elderly people to live in their own homes instead of nursing homes and to have a major decision-making role in their health-care services. Although not incorporated as a cooperative, the statewide non-profit network also represents a "cooperative" approach for CILs and elderly-care providers to stretch their financial resources and share technical expertise.

Thus, Access is attempting to respond to its growth over the past few years by returning the parent organization to a sharper focus on its basic mission, while at the same time forming an alliance with other organizations to ensure that disabled consumers have control over their home-care and health-care services. It's a huge step from being a small volunteer organization advocating for curb cuts and transportation services in the 1970s to becoming a statewide network of independent living centers planning to create a network of their own health maintenance organizations in the late 1990s. If they are successful, it will represent another major step in the increased consumer rights of people with disabilities.

CONCLUSION

The consumer movement among people with disabilities has come a long way during the past 25 years. The consumer-controlled centers for independent living have been the major organizational vehicle providing disability services and advocating for and protecting the rights of people with disabilities. But the rapid growth of this movement hasn't been easy or smooth. Because CILs are partially dependent on federal and state funding and because of the current wave of fiscal conservatism sweeping the country, many centers are likely to be in for some difficult times ahead.

What are some of the most important lessons we can derive from this consumer movement? One is that a small number of dedicated individuals can make a difference. The origins of the movement can be traced back to one university campus and a group of students with quadriplegia intent on gaining equal access to education, transportation, independent housing, and other basic needs for themselves and other people with disabilities. These young people and the many others who joined and expanded the independent living movement brought into being a new kind of consumer organization in the United States and in many other countries.

A second lesson is that the successes of the consumer movement and the civil rights movement among people with disabilities were mutually supportive parts of the same larger process. Without Section 504 of the 1973 Rehabilitation Act, without explicit inclusion of CILs as eligible recipients of funds in the Rehabilitation Act of 1978, and without the

Americans With Disabilities Act of 1990, there would be no independent living movement as we know it today. On the other hand, without the determined efforts of thousands of people with disabilities and their supporters, these civil rights breakthroughs would not have occurred.

A third lesson is one with which the independent living movement is still grappling. The core issue of the movement is equal access – creating a social and physical environment in which people with a variety of disabilities can make choices about their lives and exercise the same rights as nondisabled people. But there are financial costs to this equality – costs in redesigning the man-made environment, transportation costs, attendant-care costs, and the costs of providing the kinds of support services provided by CILs. There are also financial costs in **not** providing equal access. In particular, it's far more expensive on average to keep a disabled person in an institution than for that person to live in an apartment and receive attendant-care services. It also costs society far less to have people with disabilities earning an income than relying primarily on Supplemental Security Income (SSI) payments.

In the current political climate, however, there's a tendency to look more at short-term costs that can be cut rather than at longer term savings that will be lost. Given the current cost-cutting myopia of public officials at all levels, the "soft services" provided by independent living centers are particularly vulnerable. This urge to reduce costs has happened before. Witness the efforts during the Carter administration to water down the equal rights provisions of the Rehabilitation Act, or the major reductions of CIL budgets during the early years of the Reagan administration in 1980 – for example, the 70 percent cut in the Berkeley center's budget.

The lesson for the independent living movement is that the fickleness of public financial support needs to be countered by centers having a diversified financial base. Berkeley has substantially increased its private financial support. Alpha One has an entrepreneurial strategy to generate revenue from some of its services and from its for-profit subsidiary, Wheelchairs Unlimited. Access to Independence is generating revenue from its personal-care service program and intends to increase its financial stability through its HMO joint venture. Independent living advocates interviewed for this chapter consistently warned about the complacency that can set in when a center has relied heavily on state or federal funding for a long period of time. This dependency can lull a CIL director and board into assuming that the public money will always be there. If these sources of funding are threatened, as they are in the mid-1990s, the strategy is often to go to Washington or the state capitol and lobby to have them reinstated. There's nothing wrong with this strategy, these spokespeople maintain, as long as it's not the only strategy. In their eyes, diversified sources of support are the only means to provide long-term stability for the centers.

The independent living movement represents by far the fastest growing consumer movement in the second half of the 20th century. Who would have imagined the sweeping changes that have taken place in just 25 years in improved civil rights and access of people with disabilities to day-to-day life in American society? In particular, who would have imagined that these vast changes would have been brought about by the leadership of an as yet unheard of type of organization called centers for independent living, in which disabled people themselves constitute the majority of the board of directors and staff? The overwhelming message of this movement is that people can make a difference when they band together cooperatively to assert their rights and to meet their needs as consumers.

ACKNOWLEDGMENTS

Deborah Altus, Co-op Access Project, Univ. of Kansas, Lawrence, KS
Bob Deist, Access to Independence, Madison, WI
Tom Hamilton, Wisconsin Department of Health and Social Services, Madison, WI
Dan Johnson, Wisconsin Department of Health and Social Services, Madison, WI
Owen McCusker, Access to Independence, Madison, WI
Sue Massara, Center for Independent Living, Berkeley, CA
Michael Mayer, Summit Independent Living Center, Missoula, MT
Kris Olsen, Co-op Directory Services, Minneapolis, MN
Laurel Richards, ILRU Research and Training Center, Houston, TX
Steve Tremblay, Alpha One, Portland, ME.

REFERENCES

Altus, Deborah. 1995. **Consumer Co-ops: A Resource Guide for Consumers with Disabilities.** Lawrence, KS: The Co-op Access Project, Univ. of Kansas. *(An excellent source of information for co-ops, non-profits and small businesses on how to be more accessible to people with disabilities.)*

Leon, Joan et al. 1995. "Saying Goodbye to a Civil Rights Giant." *Impact.* Oakland, CA: World Institute on Disability, Summer and Spring.

Levy, Chava Willig. 1988. **A People's History of the Independent Living Movement.** Lawrence, KS: Research and Training Center on Independent Living, Univ. of Kansas.

Pelka, Fred. 1995. "Ed Roberts, 1939 - 1995." *Mainstream.* May: 24.

Shapiro, Joseph. 1994. **No Pity: People with Disabilities Forging a New Civil Rights Movement.** New York: Times Books. *(An informative and moving history of cooperative action by people with disabilities.)*

CHAPTER 8.

COMMUNITY DEVELOPMENT CREDIT UNIONS:
CITIZENS INVESTING IN THEIR COMMUNITIES

Credit unions are financial cooperatives that trace their roots back to mid-19th century Europe, where farmers and workers struggling through hard economic times banded together to provide themselves the credit they so badly needed to survive. Today's credit unions, now numbering about 12,000 in the United States, still offer their members a way to take control of their financial lives. But modern credit unions are about much more than extending credit. Many have evolved into full-service financial institutions offering everything from ATM service to money market accounts.

Along with the shift to more sophisticated financial services has come a renewed interest in the credit union movement during recent years in reaching out to people of marginal financial means. Community development credit unions are the form that this outreach takes. By definition, more than half (at least 51 percent) of the membership of these credit unions must be people who have low incomes. The Federation of Community Development Credit Unions, formed in 1974, has been a major impetus behind the growth of community development credit unions, having raised more than $5 million in deposits from the private sector since 1984.

Community development credit unions got an additional infusion of energy and support in 1993 when President Bill Clinton introduced the Community Development Banking and Financial Institutions Act. This law aims to help launch 100 new community development financial institutions within the next five years, many of which could be credit unions.

In this chapter, we'll look at three community development credit unions that are diverse in their origins and geographic locations, but that all aim to give their members more financial clout – as well as hope.

LOOKING FOR A NEW MODEL

On July 15, 1993, Tim Bazemore stood on the White House lawn telling a crowd of bankers and community development specialists that poor minorities could build enterprises, create jobs and instill confidence in their future. Bazemore wasn't just speaking theoretically. He'd witnessed such accomplishments firsthand as founder and general manager of Workers Owned Sewing Company, which was formed when a group of employees decided to buy out the company they worked for and thus save their jobs. At that time, Self-Help Credit Union had been there to give them financial backing. Today Workers Owned Sewing Company has annual sales of more than $2 million, and its workforce has grown from 10 to 70-plus, making it the second largest employer in rural Bertie County. What's more, Bazemore emphasized to his White House audience, the work done by Self-Help to spur that kind of economic growth in his state's low-income communities could serve as a model for the entire country.

As Bazemore spoke, a noted member of the audience nodded in agreement and then rose to take his turn at the speaker's podium. In his speech, President Bill Clinton announced his new legislation, called the Community Development Banking and Financial Institutions Act, which aimed to spark the emergence of community development financial institutions, such as Self-Help, all across the United States.

This was an issue that had been close to Clinton's heart since his days as governor of Arkansas. Back then, two economic development projects had captured his imagination. One was a system of flexible manufacturing networks and small cooperatives in northern Italy. The other was the Grameen Bank in Bangladesh, which had taken the idea of lending circles and created a way to revolutionize the lives of the poor.

Now, Clinton said, it was time to bring such models to life right here in the United States. The Community Development Banking and Financial Institutions Act was a key first step. Although Congress later scaled back the President's budget, thus funding only 100 development financial institutions rather than the 300 Clinton had envisioned, the program did get rolling.

BEGINNING WITH A BAKE SALE

While the legislation was being hammered out, advocates pointed to Self-Help as an example of what could be done if such a law were passed. The credit union's story starts back in 1980, when husband-and-wife team Martin Eakes and Bonnie Wright decided they wanted to do something about the linked problems of race and poverty in North Carolina. Toward that end, they founded the Center for Community Self-Help as a non-profit organization. Initially the center provided technical assistance and training to workers displaced by plant shutdowns. The goal was to help workers form cooperatives and employee-owned companies.

Eakes and Wright based their project on the Mondragon cooperatives in the Basque region of Spain, where a network of cooperatives had revived a dying regional economy. Indeed, the cooperatives had transformed the region into an economic powerhouse in the flourishing post-Franco era in Spain. Today the Mondragon Cooperative Corporation employs more than 25,000 worker-members, is one of the top 10 corporations in Spain and tallies billions of dollars in international sales annually.

However, Eakes and Wright discovered that the engine that gave Mondragon its power was missing in North Carolina and was stalling development of worker co-ops. That element was access to capital. For the Mondragon cooperatives, the Caja Laboral (or "Workers Bank") furnished the necessary capital to launch successful ventures. Thus, Eakes and Wright decided, their next step was to create a Caja for North Carolina.

In 1984, the couple organized the Self-Help Credit Union and Self-Help Ventures Fund (a fund-raising arm) with $77 raised from a bake sale. It was a small start, viewed by many as merely idealistic. Yet Eakes and Wright had plenty of proof of the need for credit among North Carolina's poor. Through the help of many others who believed in the credit union's philosophy and purpose, the assets began to grow. Groups such as Co-op America, a Washington-based national organization, told its 45,000 members about the work that Self-Help was doing in North Carolina. Those members and others around the country invested deposits in Self-Help. Religious institutions and other supportive organizations also became depositors. By pooling their resources at the credit union, people felt they would create the type of financial institution the country so badly needed.

Thus, Self-Help was the first community development credit union to take its case to the country and to prove that, with the right model and a solid record, the deposits would flow in.

In 1985, the United Nations named Self-Help as one of the 20 most successful rural development programs in the United States. That same year President Reagan's Task Force on Capital Mobilization for Low-Income Communities also cited Self-Help as a national model.

From there, Self-Help's achievements began to spiral. In 1987, it became the first statewide development financial institution in the country. As a result of its efforts, Self-Help received its first grant of $2 million from the North Carolina General Assembly in 1988. In 1990, the Small Business Administration and Fannie Mae approved Self-Help as a participant in their programs. Meanwhile, the resources kept growing and the customers kept coming. By 1992, Self-Help had become recognized as a new model of economic development for this country. The credit union is proud of the part it played in designing Clinton's version of the Community Development Banking and Financial Institutions Act.

As of 1995, Self-Help ranked as the largest community development credit union in the United States, with assets of $77 million. Not bad for a small effort launched by $77 in bake sale proceeds a little more than a decade earlier. The credit union now operates statewide through five regional offices that serve its members, including minorities, women, rural residents and low-income citizens of North Carolina. These are people who often encounter barriers to obtaining credit from traditional lenders.

Self-Help's belief is that ownership allows people to improve their economic position, and that, conversely, lack of wealth can prevent individuals from improving, or even maintaining, their standard of living. With that philosophy in mind, the credit union has loaned nearly $40 million to small businesses and non-profit organizations, thus helping to create more than 4,000 jobs and more than 2,000 child-care spaces. In addition, it has loaned more than $30 million to help some 600 North Carolina families buy their own homes. It's worth noting that Self-Help's cumulative loan losses, as of year-end 1994, totaled less than 1 percent, a rate comparable to conventional lenders.

Another key to Self-Help's effectiveness is that it realizes no one organization can meet all the credit needs of poor North Carolinians. Therefore, Self-Help has joined forces with other non-profits, foundations and government agencies to generate millions of dollars for additional lending. With its history of growth and success, Self-Help has become a credible advocate for public policies and practices that help low-income people improve their lives.

WHEN THE BANKS SHUT YOU OUT

In the 1970s, Santa Cruz, CA, was a hive of activity focused on environmental causes and economic and social change. Many community activists were searching for capital to fund their various efforts. But the local banking institutions had little sympathy for the motley crew that ranged from surfers to socialists. In turn, the activists decided that if the local banks wouldn't lend them the money they needed to grow their enterprises, they'd start their own financial institution. Such an institution, they reasoned, would understand what they were doing and serve as a tool for achieving the progress they envisioned.

Thus, the Santa Cruz Community Credit Union came into existence in 1977. More than the other community development credit unions founded during the same period, the credit union in Santa Cruz placed its major emphasis on loans to community businesses and non-profits. The original intent was to lend 60 percent of the credit union's resources for community development and 40 percent for personal loans. For years, Santa Cruz CCU was the bane of the credit union regulators. The latter would say, "You can't do this," and the credit union would respond, "But that's what our member borrowers want."

Eventually, the regulators put a cap on the commercial loan activity of the credit union. However, through its persistence, the credit union still makes more commercial loans proportionately than any other credit union in the United States. "Small business lending is absolutely in line with the credit union mission," says Jeff Wells, vice president of community development and lending at Santa Cruz CCU. "The Credit Union National Association's slogan is 'People Helping People.' And small businesses are an integral part of the communities credit unions are supposed to serve." The Santa Cruz CCU board is proud that it has continued to lend for social change without short-changing its borrowers or compromising its responsibilities as a well-run financial institution.

The credit union's mission statement clearly and succinctly outlines its philosophy:

The Santa Cruz Community Credit Union is a savings and lending cooperative, open to all county residents. We are working to promote social and economic change in Santa Cruz County. The Credit Union is democratically owned and controlled by its members. The Credit Union recirculates savings within the county by making loans to members. In our community development lending, we encourage democracy – the control of the local economy by the people who live here. The Credit Union's highest priority is to meet the needs of low-income people through the development of small business, cooperatives, worker-controlled businesses, non-profits and organizations improving the quality of life in the county. In our personal lending and in our other services, we help our members meet their real financial needs. Together we are people who make a difference.

Santa Cruz CCU's growth depends on staying in touch with its members. Over time, the organization has created financial and loan programs to meet the demand coming from its low- and moderate-income members. The credit union also knows its members' needs for personal loans, home loans and business loans. Unlike banks that try to develop financial services to "sell" to their customers, the credit union focuses on providing the services its members want to buy.

In line with that approach, Santa Cruz CCU was one of the first community development credit unions to realize that it needed to be a full-service financial institution in order to best meet members' needs.

Therefore, the credit union now offers savings accounts, checking accounts, IRAs, ATMs, credit cards, banking by phone, and consumer, real estate and community loans. Most members look upon Santa Cruz CCU as their primary financial institution. In 1995, the credit union performed more than 450,000 transactions and cleared 550,000 checks. As a result of its professional leadership, Santa Cruz CCU is the third largest community development credit union in the United States. As of early 1996, it had more than $20 million in deposits and 6,000 members.

During its first 19 years, the credit union loaned more than $35 million to small businesses, non-profits and cooperatives. Business loans are important to the community economy, as the vast majority of workers at these borrower enterprises are low-income. Here are just a few of Santa Cruz CCU's achievements to date:

• Lending to women- or minority-owned businesses. This has been one of the credit union's top priorities. In the last three years alone, it has issued 137 loans totaling $4.7 million to these businesses.

• Funding small business startups. In just the last three years, the credit union has made community development loans totaling $9.8 million, which resulted in 1,105 new or saved jobs. The delinquency rate hovers at an acceptable 1 percent to 2 percent.

• Supporting affordable housing. Santa Cruz CCU has provided bridge and long-term financing for a number of projects. Among them: three low-income, limited equity mobile home park cooperatives; two apartment co-ops; a residential home for HIV-positive people; two homeless shelters; a community residence for severely mentally retarded people; a battered women's shelter; and a housing project for low-income elderly persons.

• Financing environmentally sound projects. The credit union has loaned more than $3 million and given other financial support to some 50 farmers and farmer cooperatives who practice organic farming methods. Other loan recipients have included natural foods stores, environmental non-profit organizations and small businesses engaged in environmentally sound practices.

• Lending to community groups. These have included diverse organizations, such as art and theater groups, drug abuse programs, health clinics, child care centers and many more.

• Community development loan programs. The credit union has two subsidiaries that are also actively involved in community development projects. These have included housing for low-income elderly, loan programs for small businesses, loan programs for child care providers serving low-income children and many others.

Clearly, the record speaks for itself. Santa Cruz CCU continues to fulfill the mission it set for itself nearly two decades ago. Within its community, there were many who had been shut out of the local economy. This coastal resort community has plenty of wealth, high-priced homes and fancy restaurants. But for the low-income people who work to keep Santa Cruz working, it is a world of high rents and expensive living costs.

Of the many financial institutions in the community, the credit union is the only one that understands these people's needs and aspirations. By helping the entrepreneurs and the non-profits that work to build a better society, the credit union is funding opportunity. That puts the Santa Cruz Community Credit Union squarely in the heart of its community.

CREDIT GROWS IN BROOKLYN

Central Brooklyn used to be a bad scene getting worse. It was full of abandoned buildings, marginal businesses, high unemployment and rampant hopelessness among its residents. But a group of young leaders decided it was time to try a different approach to their community's economic development. In 1984, they formed the Central Brooklyn Partnership, comprised of people from economic development organizations and local churches. It was a first step toward revitalizing the community they all called home. They took another big step on April 17, 1993, when they opened the doors of the Central Brooklyn Federal Credit Union – the first credit union chartered under the Clinton administration's new Community Development Banking and Financial Institutions Act.

The main impetus for opening the credit union was the closing of many of the banks in the area. Local residents were particularly hard hit when the African-American-owned Freedom National Bank collapsed in 1990 and closed down its two Brooklyn offices. A study conducted in the late 1980s showed that at that time a sum of $629 million was on deposit from the Central Brooklyn area. However, the research also showed that for every dollar on deposit, only one cent was being reinvested in the area. Shorn of the mother's milk of capital, the community lacked a critical tool to succeed. Their capital was leaving their community and being used for development elsewhere. As each bank closed or merged, the 700,000 mostly African-American residents of Central Brooklyn saw their money going farther and farther afield and clearly not staying at home.

In the economic vacuum created by institutional abandonment, two young leaders saw the problem and spotted the opportunities. In 1989, Mark Winston Griffith was the assistant director of the Crown Heights Neighborhood Improvement Association. He took the initiative to call together the community groups who eventually created the Central Brooklyn Partnership. Griffith now serves as the executive director of the Partnership and in that role also became the co-founder and president of the credit union.

The second young visionary is Errol T. Louis, who was the associate director of the National Federation of Community Development Credit Unions, an organization based in Brooklyn. Louis had written convincingly about the importance of local financial institutions as the key to economic development. As co-founder of Central Brooklyn FCU, Louis developed and executed the credit union's organizing campaign and wrote the business plan approved by the National Credit Union Administration (NCUA), the credit union regulatory agency. Louis is now the manager and treasurer of the credit union.

Today the key challenge facing Central Brooklyn FCU lies in convincing the area's residents to look toward the future in a new way and to shift their money to the credit union. Currently the credit union has more than 4,000 members and nearly $5 million in assets. It's the fastest growing financial institution in New York City and is gaining 200 new members each month. As quickly as it can, the credit union is adding to the range of services it provides. Its services include savings and checking accounts, check cashing, utility bill payments, financial management workshops. and personal and business loans. When it began, the NCUA placed a number of loan limitations on the credit union to assure its stability. Slowly, those restrictions are being raised, which allows the credit union to provide more services to its members. In the three years it has been in business, Central Brooklyn FCU already has made more than $1.5 million in loans to members. The average loan size is about $4,000.

The credit union views itself as both a financial institution and an advocate. "In this community," Griffith points out, "we have always been concerned with political, cultural and economic development. And the credit union was a natural evolution of our thinking to create a power base, so people who live here and work here could actually participate in the empowerment of their community." Both Griffith and Louis see the credit union as a continuum from the civil rights and black power eras. They both feel that economic empowerment is the next stage.

Interestingly, both Griffith and Louis have strong family ties to the Caribbean, a similarity shared by a large population of West Indians who live in this part of Brooklyn. Central Brooklyn is the largest Caribbean community in the United States. The credit union movement is strong in the Caribbean, where the idea was grafted onto the credit circles brought to the islands from Africa. General Colin Powell has mentioned the strength of the credit circles as part of the solid West Indian family structure that he benefited from while growing up. The credit union movement in the Caribbean Islands gave blacks their first chance at economic independence from the white-owned, mainly British banks.

Another idea that has been borrowed from the African culture is the "Sister's Lending Circle." This is an adult financial literacy program run by the Central Brooklyn Partnership that targets women on public assistance. Twelve participants meet once a week and share in training sessions. Each of the participants sets goals that are supported through a peer lending process called a "su-su," modeled after a West African lending circle.

The Partnership also has invested in a range of youth development program all focused on economic development. More than 600 youths now have accounts at the credit union. Soon they will have their own youth credit union.

To strengthen their community, the Central Brooklyn Partnership linked the parent non-profit, the credit union and a loan fund (run by the Partnership and with assets of more than $200,000). This combination of resources directed at economic development provides a triad of support for people and businesses. Louis believes President Clinton is looking for this type of community-based model. "We are the kind of institution," he says, "that will make the President's plan for community development financial institutions a reality." Revitalizing the inner cities will only occur when people have faith in themselves and are in control over their financial institutions.

Griffith and Louis have used their Ivy League skills to get major banking institutions in New York City to become the credit union's partners. Griffith graduated from Brown and was a Revson Fellow at Columbia, while Louis has a B.A. from Harvard and an M. A. from Yale. The two young men combined their commitment to their community with their capacity for "working the city." They have encouraged a number of banks to place deposits in the credit union. As a result, the credit union has the highest number of deposits from financial institutions of any community development credit union. Chemical Bank even donated an old bank branch office to serve as the credit union's first location.

With determination and dedication, the Central Brooklyn FCU has arrived. In just three years, it has become the largest minority-controlled community development credit union in the country. Because of its early success, it is seen as a model for other minority communities. Previous generations of minority leaders placed their focus on combating racism and inequality. As a result, our nation was changed permanently by protest and programs. But today Central Brooklyn still has tremendous needs and still represents immense poverty, while only a few miles away sit some of the richest institutions in the United States. The growing gap between rich and poor needs to be bridged to assure this country's future stability.

The busy little credit union in Central Brooklyn is one step in that direction. Griffith and Louis represent a new generation who are bringing their skills home. They are searching for new models to rebuild their communities and for new ways to convince their neighbors that they can invest in themselves and their community by putting their money in their credit union.

CONCLUSION

Credit unions have had a long tradition of following the "people helping people" philosophy. Now community development credit unions are taking that effort to a new level, reaching more people who have felt a lack of financial power in the past.

Community development credit unions, however, are not institutions bent on "doing good." They are power bases for helping people make things happen – whether it be a group of workers who want to buy the company they work for, an individual who's trying to launch a small business, or a group of community residents who need funds to start a cooperative. Indeed, community development credit unions can be the vital link that allows other co-op projects, such as those described in other chapters of this book, to become realities.

While other financial institutions too often turn their backs, community development credit unions make investing in their communities their number one priority. Oftentimes, as we have seen in this chapter, they are investing in communities that others long ago gave up on. Of course, community development credit unions can't do it all alone. Partnerships are a key in revitalizing communities. By teaming up with other non-profits, government agencies, foundations and so on, community development credit unions are making progress in turning bad situations around – one community at a time.

ACKNOWLEDGMENTS

Patricia Brownell, Executive Director, Credit Union Foundation, Madison, WI

Martin Eakes, President and CEO, Self-Help, Durham, NC

Cyndy Falgout, Communications Director, Self-Help, Durham, NC

Errol Louis, Treasurer and Manager, Central Brooklyn Federal Credit Union, Brooklyn, NY

Cliff Rosenthal, Executive Director, National Federation of Community Development Credit Unions, Brooklyn, NY

Jeff Wells, Vice President, Community Development and Lending, Santa Cruz Community Credit Union, Santa Cruz, CA

REFERENCES AND SOURCES

Isbister, John. 1994. **Thin Cats: The Community Development Movement in the United States.** Davis, CA: Center for Cooperatives, Univ. of California.

Caftel, Brad. 1978. **Community Development Credit Unions: A Self Help Manual.** Berkeley, CA: National Economic Development Law Project.

Santa Cruz Community Credit Union. 1995. *1994 Annual Report.* Santa Cruz, CA

Self-Help. 1995. *Biennial Report 1993-1994.* Durham, NC

PART III:
COOPERATIVE PATHS
TO COMMUNITY DEVELOPMENT

CHAPTER 9.

THE GREEN BAY PACKER MODEL:
COMMUNITY-OWNED TEAMS

In addition to being an active form of recreation for tens of millions of Americans, sports is also a major industry. The combined market value of the 113 major league baseball, basketball, football and hockey teams in the United States and Canada is estimated at about $13 billion. This chapter looks at the ownership of professional sports teams, with a particular focus on teams owned by the communities in which they play.

The Green Bay Packers have been community-owned since 1923. How did this happen? Why haven't other major league teams followed suit? The chapter also examines the "transitional" community ownership of the Kansas City Royals and the successful, long-term, local ownership of seven minor league baseball teams.

The key issue of this chapter is the anomaly of major league sports teams in the United States and Canada having strong, regional fan and local government support, but, with one exception, no reciprocal commitment to their communities. The chapter poses the question: Can the scattering of major and minor league examples of community ownership pave the way for future relationships between teams and local communities that are characterized by mutual support, long-term commitment and cooperation?

DR. WEBBER KELLY, GREEN BAY PACKER HALL OF FAMER

E.G. Nadeau's great uncle, Dr. Webber Kelly, died in 1951. He was inducted into the Green Bay Packer Hall of Fame in 1994. Dr. Kelly never played or coached a down of football in his life, although he was the team physician and a member of the Packers' executive committee during the 1920s, '30s and '40s.

Being the team doctor and a director, however, were not the reasons for his induction. This honor was based on the fact that he played a key role in keeping the team in Green Bay in the early 1920s and again in the

1930s – two crisis periods when the Packers were on the brink of folding or leaving town. Uncle Webber was one of five men who conceived the idea of making the Packers a community-owned team and who turned this idea into a reality.

FOOTLOOSE AND LOYALTY-FREE

Before examining the Packers' ownership structure, let's take a brief look at the economics of the 113 major league baseball, basketball, hockey and football teams in the United States and Canada. The cumulative financial impact of these teams is impressive – almost $6 billion in total team revenue in 1994 from gate receipts, other stadium revenue (luxury boxes, parking and concessions), media revenue, and earnings from licensing and merchandise.

But the importance of professional sports in our economy is far less than the hype and glitter might indicate. Allen Sanderson argues this case convincingly in his article "Bottom-Line Drive." According to Sanderson, the average major league baseball team generates much less revenue in a year – about $70 million – than a mid-size department store. Full-time employment for all 28 major league baseball teams combined, including the players, is less than 2,000. Thus, in reality, professional sports teams are small-to-medium-sized businesses, not the large, powerful corporations they appear to be.

The dominant position of professional sports in our society is primarily cultural and psychological, not economic. Most American men, a sizable minority of American women and many of our children of both genders avidly follow one or more pro sports teams, usually teams that are based in or near our hometowns or the cities where we grew up. In this chapter, we won't analyze the origins of this sports fixation. Suffice it to say that pro sports teams (and college and high school teams as well) appear to be an extension of the fan's individual and community identity. If my team does well, it's a source of personal and civic pride. If it does poorly, I might be upset, but I can grouse about it with my friends, neighbors and workmates and, thus, even losses can lead to community interaction. And, of course, following sports is an escape. Personal troubles and community problems disappear, at least temporarily, in the theater of a sports event.

There is an important irony in the relationship between fans and the teams they support. With few exceptions, it's a very imbalanced relationship. Local sports followers and local governments identify closely with local teams and support them over the long haul. The large majority of professional sports teams have shown no such commitment to their communities. In an article entitled "The Shakedown," *Sports Illustrated* reported in 1995 that 39 professional sports team owners were threatening to move their teams to other cities if they didn't get what they wanted. The concessions demanded were usually in the form of new or renovated stadiums, more luxury boxes, or better lease arrangements. In other words, more than one-third of professional sports owners were simultaneously blackmailing their communities with variations on the theme of "Give us what we want or we're outta here."

Historically, the sale and relocation of teams has a similar dynamic to the trading of player cards. The Boston Braves became the Milwaukee Braves and now are the Atlanta Braves. The Seattle Pilots are now the Milwaukee Brewers. The Minnesota Lakers are now the Los Angeles Lakers. (Did you ever wonder why a team on the Pacific Ocean is called the Lakers?) The Oakland Raiders became the Los Angeles Raiders and then went back to Oakland. The Cleveland Rams became the Los Angeles Rams and, thanks to a $20 million cash payment and the offer of a new stadium, became the St. Louis Rams in 1995. The Cleveland Browns are off to Baltimore in 1996. The Seattle Seahawks may go to Los Angeles; the Houston Oilers to Nashville. And on it goes.

Who gains from these moves and threatened moves? Certainly not the fans and municipalities left behind. It can also be persuasively argued that many of the "winning" communities are financial losers as well, having paid far more to entice or retain the teams than they receive in economic benefits.

It doesn't have to be this way. In the remainder of this chapter we look at how the home team can truly become the home team. We provide several examples illustrating how teams and their communities can have a cooperative relationship rather than the current lopsided one in which footloose owners call the shots.

ONE TEAM THAT WON'T PACK UP AND LEAVE

The Green Bay Packers are the only major league sports franchise in the United States and Canada that is owned by the community in which it plays. The team has been community-owned for more than 70 years. With fewer than 200,000 residents in the metropolitan area, Green Bay, Wisconsin is the smallest community in North America with a professional sports franchise. Despite the small size of its home market, the Packers rank in the top 20 percent of all major league sports teams in terms of its franchise value. Since the team almost doubled the number of luxury boxes at Lambeau Field prior to the 1995 season to 193 and all of these boxes are sold, the financial picture is even better in 1995 and 1996. There are 20,000 people on a waiting list to buy season tickets in a stadium with a seating capacity of 60,000. It's common for season tickets to be willed from one generation to the next and to be hotly contested in divorce proceedings.

What might be surprising is that the current economic strength and popularity of the Packers come despite the team's not winning a National Football League championship or a Super Bowl since 1967, the last year Vince Lombardi was coach. In fact, there have been some downright mediocre seasons over the past 28 years. And yet the community has remained loyal, if sometimes disgruntled, during this long dry spell. Part of this patience stems from a long tradition of winning football in Green Bay up through the Lombardi era – 11 world championships between 1929 and 1967, including the first two Super Bowls. But a good part of this loyalty through the lean years is due to the fans' commitment to *their* team.

Green Bay's formula works. How did it come about? Why haven't other communities adopted this obviously successful approach?

The Packers have been owned by their community almost since the beginning of professional football. Green Bay fielded a citywide, semi-pro team that played other cities in the Midwest beginning in 1896. The team was christened the Packers in 1919 because it was sponsored that year by the Indian Packing Corporation, a meatpacking company. The organizers of that team were E.L. "Curly" Lambeau, who was both coach and a star player and had played college football for Notre Dame, and George Whitney Calhoun, the team manager and a reporter for the Green Bay Press Gazette.

The team was undercapitalized from the start. After a couple of rained-out games and weak attendance in 1922, the Packers were already on the verge of bankruptcy. A small group of influential citizens (including Dr. Kelly) who didn't want to see the team go away, held a series of meetings in 1922 and 1923 to figure out how to raise the necessary capital to keep them in town. The first effort at fund raising did not go well, so the organizers regrouped. They decided to reorganize the team as a non-profit organization to be called the Green Bay Packer Corporation. All the profits generated by the corporation were to be turned over to a local American Legion chapter. This struck a positive note in the immediate post-World War I era. The organizers were able to sell 1,500 shares in the form of $5 stock certificates at the beginning of the 1923 season and, thus, were able to save the team and, inadvertently, establish a new form of professional sports ownership in the United States. To quote the Packer historian, Larry Names:

"Everyone... did his part to write this incredible chapter in the histories of Green Bay, free enterprise, social conscience (after all, man cannot live by bread alone; he must also have football), the National Football League, and sports in general.... Their task was monumental, but they varied not from it.... [T]hey refused to accept defeat and renewed their efforts to put Green Bay on the NFL map for good."

The Packers faced two other financial crises over the next 30 years. The team went into receivership in 1933 in large part due to low ticket sales resulting from the Depression. In order to get out from under $19,000 in debt, the Green Bay Packer Corporation was dissolved in 1935. Green Bay Packers, Inc., also a non-profit organization, succeeded the old corporation. Green Bay Packers, Inc. was capitalized with 600 shares of no par (e.g., no financial value) common stock at a price of $25 per share. A local American Legion post continued to be the team's financial beneficiary.

The third financial crisis in the Packers' history came in the late 1940s and 1950. Its primary cause was the formation of the All-American Conference and a bidding war for players that sharply increased the operating expenses of NFL teams, including the Packers. In 1949, the Packers held an intrasquad game on Thanksgiving as a fund-raiser to reduce the Team's estimated $90,000 debt. The event was successful thanks to 500 volunteers who sold tickets for the game. The intrasquad game, however, was not enough to turn the corner on the Packers' financial woes. In 1950, the stockholders of Green Bay Packers, Inc. agreed to conduct another stock sale drive, this time raising $125,000 through the sale of 5,000 shares priced at $25 per share. The maximum number of shares allowed per shareholder was 200 in order to avoid any one individual or company having too much control.

The structure of the Packers since 1923 has undergone few changes even though the old Packer organization was dissolved and a new one formed in 1935. One exception is that the 1,500 shares of voting stock in the old corporation were no longer in effect after the dissolution. There were about 4,600 voting shares remaining in 1995, owned by approximately 1,900 shareholders, the large majority of whom are located in the Green Bay area. These shares entitle their owners to voting rights, but, because it is a non-profit corporation, the shares have no financial value. There is an annual stockholder meeting at which a 20-member board of directors is elected. The board meets five times a year and elects a seven-member executive committee. Of the directors and officers, only the elected team president receives a salary.

The Packers don't meet the definition of a formal cooperative because the shareholders control the corporation but don't "own" it. In most respects, however, it operates like a co-op. It has a broad base of shareholders, none of whom control a large enough block of stock to dominate decision-making. The corporation is operated to provide a service to the community, rather than to make a profit for its owners. It's difficult to imagine the circumstances under which the team would ever leave Green Bay. If this approach to professional sports has worked so well in Green Bay, why haven't any of the other 112 major league sports franchises adopted this model?

A ROYAL LEGACY IN KANSAS CITY

Broad-based community ownership is not the only way to establish and maintain a cooperative relationship between a sports team and the community in which it plays. Prior to his death in 1993, Ewing Kauffman put together a plan to donate the Royals to the Greater Kansas City Community Foundation in order to ensure that the team would stay in Kansas City. The plan was a complicated one, establishing a limited partnership of five investors to run the team and issuing nonvoting stock to the Foundation. A key factor in this deal was the need for a ruling by the Internal Revenue Service that a professional sports franchise could be run as a "charity." A favorable IRS ruling finally came in the summer of 1995, thus legitimating Kauffman's donation. A further complication of the deal was the stipulation by other major league baseball owners that the team had to be sold to a private owner by the year 2000. In other words, the owners were willing to accept non-profit ownership in Kansas City as a transitional, not as a permanent, option.

The strategy of Kauffman and his trustees is to use the next few years to strengthen the Royals' financial position and, thus, make the team a more attractive purchase for a new local owner. If this strategy fails, the sale of the club will be opened up to nonlocal buyers. Because of his commitment to the Kansas City area, Kauffman entered into a long-term stadium lease in the early 1990s on behalf of the Royals. The lease doesn't expire until 2015 and was designed to make it very expensive for any subsequent owner to relocate the team to another community.

Kauffman's efforts to keep the Royals in Kansas City may or may not be successful. They provide an example of how a community-spirited owner can creatively attempt to keep a team locally owned even in the face of poor financial performance and obstacles put in his way by other club owners.

Joan Kroc, former owner of the San Diego Padres and the widow of Ray Kroc, the founder of the McDonald's hamburger chain, also attempted to guarantee that the Padres stayed in town. However, her attempt to donate the club to the city of San Diego in 1987 was foiled by a veto by her fellow major league baseball team owners. The club has since been sold to other private investors and remains in San Diego, for now.

Other teams, such as the Milwaukee Brewers, the Baltimore Orioles and the Cincinnati Reds, have long-term stadium leases that greatly reduce their likelihood of leaving town. In a number of cases these "agreements" have amounted to little more than blackmail.

The agreement between the Milwaukee Brewers and the state of Wisconsin, entered into in October 1995 and being revised in the summer of 1996, is a case in point. The state agreed to put up about $160 million for a new stadium with a retractable roof and luxury boxes. The Brewers' share was $90 million – $50 million in debt financing and the remainder to come primarily from the presale of luxury box seating and from other financial benefits of the yet-to-be-built stadium. In other words, the Brewers financed their share with no money down, although they did enter into a 25-year lease agreement. The state and the city of Milwaukee will receive no share of ownership and no direct return on their investment, although there are many indirect benefits from retaining the team in the state.

Public funds were invested directly in the purchase of the Pittsburgh Pirates and the Montreal Expos. In 1985, the Pirates were sold for $41 million, of which $26 million came from 12 private investors and the remaining $15 million came from the city of Pittsburgh. The city was barred by major league owners from receiving any equity for its investment. Similarly, the city of Montreal and the province of Quebec put up $33 million out of a total of $98 million for the purchase of the Expos. For their investment, the two governmental bodies received no share of ownership and no voice in decisions related to the club.

MAJOR LESSONS FROM THE MINOR LEAGUES

The Packers may be the only major league team in the United States and Canada that is community-owned, but it's not the only professional sports team in this category. Other excellent examples can be found in the minor leagues. One of them is located 20 miles south of Green Bay.

The Timber Rattlers are a Class A affiliate of the Seattle Mariners, playing in the Midwest League. The team is owned by the Appleton Baseball Club, Inc., founded in 1958. Like the Packers, the club is structured as a non-profit organization. In October 1995, it had 240 members who owned from 1 to 50 voting shares each at a purchase price of $50 per share. Members also pay a $25 annual fee. They elect a 21-member board of directors, who in turn elect an eight-member executive committee. Last year, the club launched a major promotion drive in conjunction with its relocation to a new stadium in Grand Chute. The club changed the team's name from the Appleton Foxes to the Wisconsin Timber Rattlers and aggressively marketed its new statewide identity. The results: an increase in the number of tickets sold from 76,000 in 1994 to 209,000 in 1995; and merchandise sales in 1995 that ranked the team number one in sales among all minor league teams in the country, thanks to an attractive logo design and brisk, national sales of caps and t-shirts. These revenues are plowed back into the stadium and the team.

At least one other club has a non-profit structure similar to the Packers and the Timber Rattlers. The Toledo Mud Hens, a Triple A baseball team, became a non-profit organization in 1965. (For you M*A*S*H buffs, Corporal Klinger was an avid fan of this team.) The club donates its profits back to the county for stadium expenses. It has set new profit records for each of the last five years.

At least three minor league baseball teams are locally owned, broad-based, for-profit corporations: the Rochester (NY) Red Wings, the Indianapolis Indians, and the Syracuse Chiefs.

The Red Wings have 8,000 shareholders who own 42,000 shares. The club has never paid a dividend and has made a commitment to Monroe County that it will not pay a dividend during the next 20 years as part of a 20-year lease agreement for the baseball stadium. The Red Wings may be a for-profit corporation in legal terms, but their overriding concern has been keeping the Red Wings in Rochester rather than turning a profit. All three of these clubs were reorganized in the late 1950s and early 1960s, when major league teams decided to cut down on the number of minor league teams they were willing to support. Many local communities had to decide whether to buy the minor league franchises in their towns or lose them. These three clubs opted for private, for-profit corporations. Some chose non-profit ownership. Others became county-owned.

The Scranton/Wilkes Barre (Pennsylvania) Red Barons and the Columbus (Ohio) Clippers are each owned by the counties where they're located. They are both Triple A teams in the International League. Two adjacent counties own and oversee the Red Barons through a Multipurpose Stadium Authority, which is operated by the counties "just as they would ... run a solid waste plant...." Both teams report having an oversight board or executive committee of some type, but, at the same time, the counties give plenty of decision-making room to the general manager and the front office.

Whether non-profit, for-profit or county-owned, all the minor league clubs mentioned above report that they are in good shape financially. The Packers and the seven minor league teams discussed here provide strong evidence that a variety of community-based forms of sports team ownership have worked well in the United States. What's more, they have stood the test of time – almost three-quarters of a century for the Packers and two to four decades for the minor league examples. So if community ownership works so well, what can we do to make it more pervasive?

A More Level Playing Field

In an interview for this chapter, Ed Garvey, an attorney and former executive director of the NFL Players Association, said, "You can't reform major league sports ownership. You have to start with new leagues." Garvey was referring to the old boys' (and, to a small extent, the old girls') network that controls each of the four major leagues and the rules they have established to maintain the current patterns of ownership. For example:

• The leagues prohibit full or partial ownership by government entities in major league sports teams, as illustrated by the Montreal Expo and Pittsburgh Pirate examples given above. This rule preventing equity investment by government bodies limits opportunities for local ownership.

• League owners as a group retain the right to prevent the sale or relocation of a team.

• Major league baseball requires that a single investor have at least 51 percent ownership of a team rather than a broad-based group (such as would be involved in community-based ownership).

It would be possible through public pressure, legal challenges in the courts and congressional changes in antitrust rules to erode some of this monopolistic power. But there is another problem besides the power of the owners: the unwillingness of communities to pursue strategies for local control. With the single exception of Green Bay, no community has gone beyond lip service when it comes to taking ownership or trying to take ownership of a major league sports team. A number of cities have shown a willingness to fork over tens of millions of dollars to build and renovate stadiums, to improve access roads and parking, and to provide direct financial incentives to owners (such as the $20 million paid by the city of St. Louis to the owner of the Rams). But none has launched a serious effort to actually own a team, nor has any city worked with local businesses and citizens to help them purchase a franchise.

Community ownership of sports teams is not a complicated issue. If a community wants a sports team and wants to insure that the team will remain there for a long time, the best ways to achieve these objectives are to own the team directly or have a long-term contract with a team owner that minimizes the likelihood of an untimely departure.

The local non-profit ownership structure of the Packers has served the fans and community of Green Bay well. When the Packers became a community-owned team, however, the cost of the franchise was a pittance compared to the cost of a team today. Local investors paid less than $150,000 to keep the team solvent and in Green Bay. Most professional sports teams today are valued at more than $100 million.

This price escalation does not mean that community ownership is impossible today. It means that communities wanting to ensure that their teams stick around must use somewhat different financial tactics than the citizens of Green Bay used. There is no magic formula for how to structure a community buyout of a team. Several options are presented below:

1. Form a non-profit corporation that is supported by public and private grants and by stock sales that allow for voting rights, but no financial return. This is similar to the Packer model.

2. Form a broad-based corporation or cooperative in which individuals and businesses purchase stock to buy the team. This is the approach used by the Rochester Red Wings.

3. Establish a public authority owned by state and/or local governments to buy the team. The Columbus Clippers are county-owned.

4. Create a corporation that includes both public and private ownership (a combination of 2 and 3).

5. Have a community-owned corporation (1, 2, 3 or 4) that joint ventures with a private owner or owners (such as the current owners of the Brewers).

It may seem daunting to raise $100 million or more from local investors. But it's really not such a big deal. A number of local and state governments have recently committed $200 million or more to building new stadiums. Most metropolitan areas have a core group of community-minded corporations, foundations and wealthy citizens who support local causes. Other businesses and sports fans can have a cumulative impact on meeting fund-raising goals. The ingredients are there. Leadership and a good financing plan are all that's needed. Of course, it also helps tremendously if the owner who is selling a team wants it to stay in town (as did Kansas City Royals owner Ewing Kauffman).

Creating and capitalizing a community-based corporation is one of two main steps necessary for success. The other step is to convince major league owners to approve the sale of the team to this new corporation. One might argue that the owners would never approve such a sale because their charter prohibits this type of broad-based ownership structure. As a former representative on the NFL owners council put it, "the owners make the rules and they can change the rules." If there were a broad sentiment among sports fans that the sale be approved, the owners may acquiesce to the pressure and let the sale go through. Then, there are always the courts. Recent court cases involving the sale or relocation of professional sports teams have tended to favor the rights of the individual owner over the rights of the league. For example, the courts upheld Al Davis' right to move the Raiders from Oakland to Los Angeles over the objections of the NFL owners association.

To a large extent then, community ownership boils down to will and commitment. If the business, political and sports leadership of a community really want to assure themselves of having a local franchise, they can do it. They can secure ownership of an established team or an expansion team, or they can enter into a long-term agreement with a team owner.

The fact that more than one-third of the 113 professional baseball, basketball, football and hockey teams in the United States and Canada recently threatened or are currently threatening to relocate if they don't get the economic concessions they want from their communities exemplifies the power and the arrogance of these owners. Local and state governments have let themselves be subjected to this kind of blackmail in exactly the same way that they have given away huge concessions to manufacturing businesses that have pitted communities against one another in no-win bidding wars.

Professional sports teams are intended to be a source of entertainment and pride for local fans and of economic and cultural benefits for local communities. Professional baseball, basketball, football and hockey can return to these simple priorities, but not until communities regain control over what has become a footloose and unaccountable ownership structure. The Packers show the benefits of local accountability, as have numerous minor league sports teams. Now it's time for more communities and more Uncle Webbers to take ownership of their sports teams.

ACKNOWLEDGMENTS

Ed Garvey, Former Executive Director, NFL Players Assoc., Madison, WI
Sally Jaeger-Altekruse, Appleton Baseball Club, Inc., Appleton, WI
Jackie Kelly, daughter of W. Webber Kelly, Green Bay, WI
Greg Lawless, Univ. of Wisconsin Center for Cooperatives, Madison, WI
Thomas J. Lutsey, Board Member, Green Bay Packers, Inc., Green Bay, WI
Jay Mortell, Diehard Packer Fan, Green Bay, WI
Judge Robert Parins, Former President, Green Bay Packers, Inc., Green Bay, WI
Marilyn Scholl, Univ. of Wisconsin Center for Cooperatives, Madison, WI

REFERENCES

Alesch, Daniel J. 1995. *The Green Bay Packers: America's Only Not-for-Profit, Major League Sports Franchise.* Milwaukee, WI: The Wisconsin Policy Research Institute, Inc. *(A well-written, concise review of the Packer's organizational structure and relationship to the community and an analysis of public policy implications.)*
Crothers, Tim. 1995. "The Shakedown." *Sports Illustrated.* June 19: 78-82.
Hewes, Havelock, and Neil Cohen. 1990. "Whose Teams Are They, Anyway?" *Sport.* July: 54-58.

Names, Larry D. 1987, 1989 and 1990. **The History of the Green Bay Packers: Books I, II and III.** Berlin, WI: Angel Press of Wisconsin. *(A painstakingly researched and very readable account of the Packers' origins and history through the Lombardi era.)*

Ozanian, Michael et al. 1995. "Suite Deals: Why New Stadiums Are Shaking Up the Pecking Order of Sports Franchises." *Financial World.* May 9: 42-56.

Sanderson, Allen. 1995. "Bottom-Line Drive." *Univ. of Chicago Magazine.* June: 18-23.

Zimbalist, Andrew S. 1992. **Baseball and Billions : A Probing Look Inside the Big Business of Our National Pastime.** New York: BasicBooks.

CHAPTER 10.

PROVIDING POWER TO RURAL COMMUNITIES

There are about 1,000 consumer-owned businesses providing electricity to some 30 million people, primarily in rural America. Most of us, even many who are member-owners of these cooperatives, know little or nothing about them – neither their history nor how they currently affect our day-to-day lives.

Electricity is not the only kind of power these co-ops deliver. They are also a means to strengthen rural economic and community power. Many rural areas are losing farms and people. Rural communities have more than their share of poverty and less than their share of jobs. Health, transportation and other services are harder to provide because the population is dispersed.

This chapter takes a brief look at the history of the rural electric cooperative movement in the United States and provides several examples of electric co-ops today that are working with their members to help provide economic empowerment as well as electricity to their communities. The chapter concludes with the observation that, because these co-ops literally network with every home and business in their communities, they have the potential to be an even more powerful force for locally based development.

WHEN THE LIGHTS CAME ON

The beginning of rural electrification in the United States is an exciting and inspiring story. For the most part, the privately owned power systems that covered most cities and suburbs during the first third of the 20th century had neglected rural America. These utilities didn't see enough profit in stringing lines from farm to farm or in providing service to other low-density communities. In 1910, a survey conducted by the National Electric Light Association concluded that the number of "farmers using electricity was almost too small to report." At that time there were approximately 6.5 million farms in the United States. In **The**

Advance of American Cooperative Enterprise: 1920-1945, Joseph G. Knapp does an excellent job chronicling the origins of rural electrification.

There were a few scattered rural electric co-ops in those early years. For example, farmers near Granite Falls, MN, piggybacked their electric co-op power lines on the city's distribution system beginning in 1914. Similar co-ops were set up in rural communities in Iowa, Idaho, Washington and elsewhere in the late 1910s and early '20s. But no systematic state or national rural electrification effort emerged until a decade later.

In the 1930s, two federal programs, the Tennessee Valley Authority and the Rural Electrification Administration, set the stage for rural electrification to spread across the entire country. President Franklin D. Roosevelt signed the Tennessee Valley Authority (TVA) Act in 1933. The TVA had a broad mandate that included developing hydroelectric power and "fostering an orderly and proper physical, economic, and social development" of the area.

In 1933 and 1934, TVA staff worked closely with the residents of Alcorn County, MS, to make reasonably priced electricity available in the county. The keys to success proved to be low-cost power from hydroelectric dams; a high percentage of households and businesses agreeing up front to join the new county electric co-op and to purchase power from it; and a loan program that spread the repayment of the co-op's start-up costs over a number of years. The Alcorn Electric Power Association was a precedent-setting success. It became the model for hundreds of other electric cooperatives that were established around the country during the following decade.

Roosevelt established the Rural Electrification Administration by executive order in 1935. The pilot successes of TVA and the Alcorn co-op were key factors in convincing the administration that rural electric cooperatives should be the vehicle for providing electricity to rural areas throughout the country. In community after community, local citizens mobilized, went door to door signing up their neighbors to become co-op members and celebrated when the power arrived. The day the lights came on was one of those never-to-be-forgotten moments for rural residents of that era.

Electricity radically transformed rural life. Electric pumps, conveyor belts, feed grinders, milking machines, refrigerators, electric stoves, radios and washing machines removed some of the menial and grueling tasks from farm work for both men and women. As Senator George Norris of Nebraska, co-sponsor of the Rural Electrification Act wrote: "I had seen first-hand the grim drudgery and grind which had been the common lot of eight generations of American farm women....Why shouldn't I be interested in ... [their] emancipation?" In only five years, from 1936 to 1940, about 600 rural electric cooperatives were formed with assistance from the Rural Electrification Administration. By 1940 about one-fourth of all farms in the United States were served by these co-ops.

EMPOWERMENT TODAY

The lights came on in most parts of rural America more than 50 years ago. Today, a system of 1,000 local rural electric cooperatives (often referred to as RECs) and 60 regional cooperatives, which generate and transmit power to the local cooperatives, serve 30 million people in 46 states. One difference from the early years is that, for the most part, the excitement and active involvement of co-op members are gone. This should not be surprising because two or three generations have passed since the organizing activities and the initial electrification in the 1930s and '40s.

Another change from the early years is in how some RECs view their mission today. Historically, many electric co-ops saw their role as providing electric power at the lowest possible price. In the past decade or so, some co-ops have broadened this role to include assisting business retention and growth, promoting job creation, and fostering other changes that provide social and economic benefits in their service areas. These co-ops are in the business of developing community and economic power as well as distributing electrical power. At the same time, the broader empowerment role of these co-ops has served to revive their members' knowledge about, and involvement in, their co-ops. The examples presented below describe rural electric cooperatives that provide both kinds of empowerment in their service areas.

POLITICAL POWER IN JACKSON COUNTY, WI

Mike Anderson is a deal maker, a man with lots of energy, always on the lookout for community and economic development projects that might benefit Jackson County, WI. Anderson has been president and CEO of Jackson Electric Cooperative since 1979. Since then he has served eight years as mayor of Black River Falls, WI (the Jackson County seat), founded and is president of the county's economic development corporation and chairs the board of the local business incubator. Anderson has acted on his strong belief that if rural electrics want to play a role in developing their communities, they must get involved in political and economic activities. This involvement goes beyond his own role as CEO. Other Jackson Electric board members and employees are also active in county affairs.

This community leadership of Jackson Electric Cooperative has contributed to the county's excellent record of bringing in outside companies, creating and expanding local businesses, and creating jobs over the last 15 years. In the early 1980s, Jackson Electric, city and county officials, and other community leaders secured federal financing for an industrial park. The two largest businesses in the park, a forest products company and an electric motor manufacturing company, employ 600 people.

The co-op also played the lead role in starting up a small business incubator in 1990. In 1996, the tenants of the incubator included a training center for Western Wisconsin Technical College, a print shop owned by the Ho-Chunk Indian Tribe, a job service office, Riverfront (a non-profit employment and training center for developmentally disabled people) and two other small businesses. Altogether, 80 people were employed in the incubator building in early 1996.

While some communities have shunned the idea of being the site of a federal or state prison, Jackson County successfully recruited a new state correctional facility because of the positive job impact it would have in the county. In 1996, the prison had about 350 employees. This number is expected to reach 500 by the year 2000.

Jackson Electric has established a close working relationship with the Ho-Chunk Indian Tribe on the business incubator and on other projects. Tribal lands are dispersed in central and west central Wisconsin. The tribe has chosen to establish its headquarters and to undertake a major expansion of its casino in Jackson County. When these two projects are completed, they will result in 500 additional jobs in the county.

The overall effect of these developments has been rapid growth and diversification of the Black River Falls and Jackson County economy. They have contributed to a reduction of the county's unemployment rate from 15.4 percent in January 1984 to 4.6 percent in November 1995. The job growth strategy of Anderson and the Jackson Electric board has worked well during the past decade and a half. The co-op's involvement in political and economic development activities and its support of diversified economic growth through business recruitment, local small business development, the new prison, and the expansion of the Ho-Chunk tribe's administrative and business activities in the county have paid off in a big way.

UTILITY PLAYER IN NORTHERN MISSOURI

The four-county region served by North Central Missouri Electric Cooperative has a number of economic strikes against it.

•The area is geographically isolated.

•There has been a major outmigration throughout the 20th century. From 1980 to 1990 alone, the population dropped from 33,700 to 29,000 a 14 percent decline.

•There is a high incidence of poverty and underemployment. A 1986 study by the Harvard University School of Public Health included three of the region's counties among the 150 counties in the United States with the highest levels of hunger.

•The hills and clay soil make farming difficult. The agricultural crisis of the early 1980s hit local farmers particularly hard because many had farms that were marginal even before the advent of astronomical interest rates, falling land values and low commodity prices.

For North Central Electric Cooperative, an electric utility dependent on the economic health of this geographic area, these trends of the post-World War II period were bad news. The co-op began to address these economic problems in earnest in 1989. One of the first things the co-op did was to come up with a clear understanding of the underlying problem and a plan of action for solving it. According to Bruce Hensley, the co-op's manager of community and government relations, neither the basic problem nor solution was an agricultural one. Hensley notes, "Only about 5 percent of our member-customers are self-sustaining farmers who make most of their incomes from farming activities. Our co-op needed to move away from the mindset that its primary constituency was farmers. We and other electric co-ops are serving rural America, not just farmers." With that understanding, the co-op focused on job retention and creation as its primary economic objective.

The results over the last five years have been impressive. Hensley projects that the number of jobs in the four-county region will increase by 3,000 between 1990 and the end of 1996. This meteoric job growth already has stopped the hemorrhaging of the region's population. After decades of decline, the population actually increased by 2,725 (more than 8 percent) between 1990 and 1995.

What were the elements of this turnaround? Con-Agra, a large food processing company, carried out a major expansion of its Healthy Choice TV dinner plant in Milan, the largest city in the region, resulting in 150 new jobs since 1992.

The biggest employment gain, however, has come from the rapid growth of Premium Standard Foods, a pork production and processing company that has established hog-raising facilities and a processing plant in the area. Premium Standard will have 2,100 employees by the end of 1996. An additional 650 jobs in transportation, feed mill operations, retail sales and other activities are also attributable to this company's recent growth.

For both the Con-Agra and Premium Standard expansions, North Central Electric Cooperative provided two key elements to help pave the way: (1) goodwill, trust and community leadership built up over years of working in the region, and (2) an ability to work with the state and the municipalities and counties in the service area in order to secure grant and loan funds for the expansions. This coordination with the public sector was crucial because many state and federal economic development dollars flow through local governments.

There are other spin-offs from the expansion of these two businesses. The majority of employees of both companies reside on farms. Their off-farm employment is often the difference between being able to stay in farming or not. Thus, an indirect effect of nonfarm employment growth is the retention of family farms.

A negative consequence of the rapid job increase is a housing shortage. Some workers commute 50 miles or more each way daily to their jobs. The need for additional housing nearer to job sites is critical. In fact, Premium Standard is delaying the start-up of a second shift because of a worker shortage. More available housing near the plant would solve the problem. North Central Co-op is playing the lead role in addressing the housing shortage. The co-op has convinced the state of Missouri to allocate to nonurban areas some of the federal and state housing funds previously restricted to large cities. As a result, Sullivan County, the site of the Premium Standard plant, will receive grants and loans for the construction of a 100-unit subdivision to be completed in 1998. The city of Milan will not provide sewer service to the subdivision because it lies just outside the city limits. The co-op will bridge the gap by creating its own sewer subsidiary to meet the needs of the new housing.

The growth of the last few years also has exacerbated the need for an improved regional water supply system. Because of a shortage of below ground water resources, wells are not a reliable source of potable water. The area needs a regional water supply lake to meet current and projected demand. Again, the co-op has played the primary leadership role in addressing this need. It has formed the North Central Missouri Regional Wholesale Water Supply District as a co-op subsidiary and in 1996 was conducting a feasibility study to determine a timetable and financing for the system.

One of the things that characterizes North Central Missouri Electric Cooperative's approach to economic and community development is its willingness to go wherever it has to in order to solve local problems. The co-op worked with other local organizations and their leaders and with private companies to address the need for more jobs. To solve housing needs, co-op representatives worked at the state level to change allocation rules and to secure housing funds. The co-op is working at the national level to change lending practices that the co-op contends discriminate against moderate income housing in rural areas. The co-op's versatile approach to economic, housing and infrastructure development in the first half of the 1990s has already helped to shift its service area from decline to growth – for the first time in this century.

PLAINLY SUCCESSFUL IN NORTH DAKOTA

In some ways North Dakota's economic problems in the late 1980s parallel those of North Central Missouri. A big difference, of course, is that North Dakota is a whole state, not a four-county region. Only four states have a lower population density than North Dakota. Its population peaked in 1930 at 681,000. The state lost 22,000 people – about 3.5 percent of its population – in the 1980s alone, leaving 630,000 residents in 1990. Six thousand farms and ranches, representing 15 percent of all the farms in the state, disappeared during the same decade, according to the 1990 U.S. census.

But some people just don't know when to quit. Among them are the management and the board of directors of the North Dakota Association of Rural Electric Cooperatives. According to Dennis Hill, executive vice president of the association as quoted in *Rural Electrification*, "If we didn't stop the decline, it seemed to us inevitable that people would start asking why we need these rural electric and telephone cooperatives."

In 1990, the association hired Bill Patrie, former director of North Dakota's economic development commission, to lead its rural development program. Within five years, 22 new "value-added" cooperatives had been incorporated in the state. Almost all received development assistance from Patrie and the electric association's rural development program. As of late 1995, these co-op ventures represented $500 million of new investment in rural North Dakota; 1,400 jobs (not including 1,000 jobs that will come on line when a state-of-the-art corn fructose plant begins operation in 1997); and investment and marketing opportunities for 4,000 farmers and ranchers from North Dakota and neighboring states. Some of these projects, such as the Dakota Growers Pasta Company and the North American Bison Cooperative, are discussed in Chapter 1.

Patrie identifies five main ingredients in North Dakota's remarkable success with cooperative development: a shared business idea, credible local leadership, an honest feasibility study, a business plan with strong member input and a successful equity investment campaign. Two additional factors should be added to this list: (1) an effective co-op development organization and personnel (Patrie, his staff and the support of the North Dakota Association of Rural Electric Cooperatives), and (2) financial support (in particular from the state of North Dakota and the St. Paul Bank for Cooperatives).

This rural development approach is different from the Jackson County and northern Missouri examples – and indeed from any other development programs sponsored by rural electrics in the United States. For one thing, it's a statewide initiative supported jointly by the electric co-ops in North Dakota. Second, it's coordinated closely with technical and financial assistance resources provided by state government. Third, it concentrates on locally based cooperative development. The program works with groups of agricultural producers to identify businesses they can own jointly to enhance the returns from their farms and ranches. These three components have produced highly impressive results after only five years.

A POWERFUL POTPOURRI OF OTHER CO-OP INITIATIVES

With 1,000 rural electric cooperatives spread around the country, there are far more good examples of co-op-sponsored community and economic development projects than there is space to write about them. Following is a sampling of development activities:

BUTLER COUNTY RURAL ELECTRIC COOPERATIVE

in northeast Iowa got into the housing business in the early 1990s. The reason? A number of rural farmsteads were unoccupied because local banks considered them to be risky investments. Bob Bauman, Butler County REC's general manager, and the co-op's board of directors chose to do something about this problem. The co-op established a low-interest revolving loan fund to make these rural houses more financially attractive to home buyers. "We needed to keep our customer base," Bauman says. "We needed to keep those acreages filled." The REC has added a full-time housing specialist to its staff and a low-interest remodeling loan program to its home buyer program. The co-op's home finance programs respond directly to the shortage of quality, affordable housing in northeast Iowa around Allison, IA.

KIT CARSON ELECTRIC COOPERATIVE

serves the rural communities around Taos, NM. The area has a large Hispanic and Native American population and, historically, has had a high incidence of unemployment. Over the last seven or eight years, the co-op has concentrated on assisting locally based business development as a means to address the chronic job shortage. The co-op took a leadership role in starting up a small business incubator in 1990. The incubator building, which is leased, now has 14 tenants and a waiting list of prospective businesses. The non-profit incubator corporation is in the process of building a larger facility of its own scheduled to open in the summer of 1996. The co-op also launched a project to assist local woodcutters and small wood-processing companies to operate their own successful businesses.

KOTZEBUE RURAL ELECTRIC COOPERATIVE

lies 30 miles above the Arctic Circle, 550 miles from Anchorage and 240 miles from the nearest Russian island in the Aleutians. The co-op is looking into the feasibility of assisting the 14 villages in its service area to install wind energy turbines to meet a major part of their energy needs. The turbines will produce both electricity and thermal energy. The villages will use diesel generators when the wind isn't blowing. The co-op is working with a Vermont-based energy company that has designed turbines to withstand the extremely harsh weather of the Arctic region. If successful, the turbines will greatly reduce the cost of energy for these primarily Native Alaskan communities. Another innovative project of the co-op is to use waste heat from its diesel generators to power an "absorption freezer" that produces up to 12 tons of ice per day for use in the fishing industry. Thus, Kotzebue's strategy for economic development is based on reducing the extremely high cost of electrical and thermal energy in its service area and turning "waste" heat into economic returns for its members.

STEELVILLE TELEPHONE COOPERATIVE

in Missouri provides a good example of a utility cooperative, other than a rural electric, that is playing a lead development role in its community. The co-op used profits from the sale of a cellular phone franchise to upgrade its technology and to form a local economic development corporation. The corporation provides seed funding to commercial and industrial projects in the Steelville area. There are about 260 rural telephone co-ops in the United States with 1.2 million members. Like their rural electric cousins, their survival and growth are tied to their service areas. Many have responded to declining populations by championing local economic growth.

PALMETTO REC, SOUTH CAROLINA
CENTRAL ELECTRIC MEMBERSHIP CORPORATION, NORTH CAROLINA

are two examples from among dozens of co-ops that have sponsored intensive community and economic development planning processes in their service areas. Working closely with local RECs, the **National Rural Electric Cooperative Association (NRECA),** based in Washington, D.C., assembles resource teams consisting of a range of housing, business, education, government and other professionals who spend several days meeting with a wide array of local citizens and touring REC service areas. Team members then prepare reports identifying the major problems they observed and heard about and, what is more important, they recommend actions to address those problems. Palmetto REC serves the popular resort community of Hilton Head. Therefore, a major part of the co-op's development strategy is to build on its locational advantages for vacation and retirement homes. Central Electric is working to strengthen the quality of K-12 schooling in its area. It's supporting a local educational foundation that provides teachers with small grants to introduce innovative features into their curricula. These are examples of national-local electric co-op partnerships designed to jump-start economic and community planning efforts. The local co-op plays the role of catalyst by bringing in expert resources to get the ball rolling.

Many rural electrics also are expanding the array of services they provide to their customer-members as part of their own business activities. Following are a few examples of these multiservice cooperatives:

EDGAR ELECTRIC COOPERATIVE ASSOCIATION,

based in Paris, IL, is providing two-way mobile radio and telephone services and water utility services in addition to the distribution of electricity.

VALLEY ELECTRIC COOPERATIVE,

headquartered in Glasgow, MT, offers telephone and computer services, cable and satellite television, and business data systems.

THE GUADELOUPE VALLEY ELECTRIC COOPERATIVE

in Gonzales, TX, provides distance learning services (interactive cable television for classroom use connecting area schools) and Med-Link services, as well as cable and satellite television. The co-op also has a financial assistance program for water supply cooperatives, operates a waste water subsidiary and is a supplier of equipment for volunteer fire departments.

These three cooperatives represent a few examples of a much larger phenomenon in which rural electrics are picking up the slack in their communities and providing an array of services not adequately provided by anyone else.

CONCLUSION

At the beginning of this chapter, we presented a brief summary of the long, proud history of rural electric cooperatives in the United States. Today, there is tremendous diversity among these cooperatives. Some co-op managers and board members see rural electrics as having the same mission as when they were founded 50 years ago – providing cheap power to farmers. Other co-op leaders, such as Bruce Hensley from North Central Missouri Electric Cooperative and Mike Anderson at Jackson Electric in Wisconsin, contend that rural electric co-ops have a very different mission from when they started. They point out that today farmers are only a small minority of their members. Agriculture is just one of many community and economic development areas in which rural electric involvement can make a difference.

The examples described above represent several different strategies being pursued by the development-oriented rural electrics. These strategies can be divided into four categories:

1. **Externally based development.** Many rural electrics, as well as many investor-owned utilities and local development corporations, have as their primary strategy for development the recruitment of businesses from outside the community. The negative name for this economic development strategy is "smokestack chasing." Most communities are not well-located to have a successful, externally based development strategy. Jackson County served by Jackson Electric Cooperative, is one of the exceptions to this rule. Interstate 94 runs right through the county. It's well-situated between the Twin Cities and Milwaukee/Chicago, making it an attractive location for both Wisconsin and Minnesota businesses seeking expansions or relocations. However, Anderson would hasten to add that attracting outside businesses is only part of Jackson Electric's strategy.

2. **Local business development.** Jackson County and the communities served by Kit Carson Rural Electric Cooperative in New Mexico both feature locally based small-business start-ups, retention and growth as key parts of their development strategy. This approach is particularly effective in rural areas that are not in a competitive position to recruit large outside businesses. It has the added advantage of creating a stable employment base that's less likely to relocate out of the community at some future date. Bill Patrie's work in North Dakota is consistent with the locally based business development approach. In his case, the emphasis is on creating new cooperatives as a specific kind of locally based business development.

3. **Multiservice strategy.** Several of the electric co-ops mentioned above have taken on expanded economic development and community service roles as direct business activities of the co-op. This is true for North Central Missouri Electric Cooperative as well as for the three examples of multiservice cooperatives presented immediately above. In this approach, the co-op may be assisting other types of economic development, but, in addition, the co-op is expanding its own role as a diversified business in the community.

4. **Participatory development planning.** In most of the examples presented above, the co-op management and the board of directors play an active role in determining and implementing the co-op's policies toward economic development. Overall, however, rural electrics have not done a good job in involving a broader group of cooperative members in these activities (although the resource team planning process developed by NRECA does build in broad community involvement in the

initial problem-identification phase). Thus, the creative ideas, skills, energy and commitment of consumer-members are largely untapped resources in the co-ops' development efforts. In the next chapter on community-based economic development, we look at a number of examples of local citizens playing an active role in identifying problems, proposing solutions and in carrying them out. This participatory approach is one that rural electrics should look at more closely, both to increase the co-ops' effectiveness in community and economic development and to increase their members' involvement and commitment.

There have been dramatic changes in the role of electric cooperatives since they brought power to rural America in the second quarter of this century. Now they are beginning to bring economic power to these communities as well. As the above examples illustrate, some co-ops are doing an excellent job of this. Because of their presence throughout rural America and because they are owned and controlled by the people and businesses they serve, electric cooperatives are in an excellent position to do a lot more.

Indeed, one could argue that electric co-ops *must* do more – in order to assure their own survival. The danger exists that if RECs, and the generation and transmission cooperatives that serve them, do not live up to their potential as economically and socially responsive, community-based organizations, they will be swallowed up by large, investor-owned utilities.

ACKNOWLEDGMENTS
Mike Anderson, Jackson Electric Cooperative, Black River Falls, WI
Frank Galant, National Rural Electric Cooperative Assoc., Washington, D.C.
Bruce Hensley, North Central Missouri Electric Cooperative, Milan, MO
Bill Patrie, North Dakota Rural Electric Cooperative Assoc., Mandan, ND
Robert Bauman, Butler County Rural Electric Cooperative, Allison, IA.

REFERENCES
Copeland, Rebecca. 1994. "Adding New Services: Diversified Co-ops Use Non-Electric Profits to Hold Down Rates." *Rural Electrification*. October: 10-17.

Karaim, Reed. 1995. "The Farmers' Firebrand: Sarah Vogel, North Dakota's Activist Agriculture Commissioner Looks to Co-ops to Revitalize the Rural Economy." *Rural Electrification*. March: 20-23.

Karaim, Reed. 1995. "Preacher on the Plains: The Story of Bill Patrie and North Dakota's Cooperative Renaissance." *Rural Electrification*. September: 20-23.

Knapp, Joseph G. 1973. **The Advance of American Cooperative Enterprise: 1920-1945.** Danville, IL: Interstate Publishers and Printers. *(Chapters 16 and 17 provide a very good and insightful overview of the origins of the rural electric system in the United States.)*

Kunka, Jill. 1991. "Looking After Your Own: A New Mexico Co-op Helps Keep Its Members Employed." *Rural Electrification.* April: 20-23.

Pence, Richard (ed.). **The Next Greatest Thing: 50 Years of Rural Electrification in America.** Washington, D.C.: National Rural Electrical Cooperative Assoc.. *(Well-illustrated history of the electric co-op movement with many interesting anecdotes and moving examples.)*

CHAPTER 11.

DEVELOPMENT AS IF PEOPLE MATTERED

Whether the issue is the quality of local schools, the availability of decent-paying jobs, parks and recreational activities, crime or affordable housing, people often feel powerless and frustrated about what happens in their neighborhoods, cities and rural communities. But things are changing. Residents of both urban and rural areas are taking action to make their communities more livable.

This chapter describes how people are taking charge of planning and development projects in their local areas. The chapter presents two different models for local involvement: the community development corporation and cooperative development planning. The former approach involves the creation of a special organization to represent the interests of local residents in development projects. The latter model provides a means for citizens to be actively engaged in planning development projects that meet community interests. This model relies on existing local governments and non-profit and for-profit organizations to implement development plans. Both approaches illustrate the creativity and effectiveness of local citizens charting the future of their own communities.

COMMUNITY DEVELOPMENT CORPORATIONS

Community development corporations (CDCs) are grass-roots organizations, providing a participatory approach to improving community life. They may be formed at a neighborhood, city, county or multicounty level to carry out economic development, housing and social service projects. CDCs should not be confused with industrial development corporations or other development organizations formed to carry out economic or housing activities by local governments, local business organizations or both. The purpose of this chapter is not to criticize these latter organizations, which quite often play a positive economic and community development role, but rather to highlight the particular features and benefits of "bottom-up" as opposed to "top-down" community planning and development.

Community development corporations are relatively new. They have their origins in the racial conflict and civil rights movement of the 1950s and '60s. Many of us have forgotten – and others of us are too young to remember – that the 1960s was a time of tremendous social and racial unrest in urban America. In 1967 alone, 150 American cities experienced civil disorders. The most serious conflict that year was in Detroit, where 43 people died, hundreds were injured and many square blocks were devastated. The Watts area of Los Angeles had suffered a similar deadly riot in the summer of 1965, with 34 people killed and $35 million in damages. In a very dramatic way, this racial violence drew attention to the terrible living conditions of poor African-Americans, Hispanic-Americans and others who saw no escape from poverty.

Even before the federal government launched its War on Poverty during the Johnson administration, a number of poor urban neighborhoods had begun to develop their own economic self-help programs. Progress Enterprises, located in a predominantly African-American neighborhood of north Philadelphia, is often cited as the first CDC. In 1962, Reverend Leon Sullivan called upon the members of Zion Baptist Church to invest $10 per month for 36 months in Progress Enterprises. Its first project was a garden apartment complex for low-income residents. This was the first of many housing, retail, manufacturing and other projects totaling millions of dollars and generating thousands of jobs that this prototype CDC has carried out in north Philadelphia.

Other early examples include: Bedford-Stuyvesant Restoration Corporation, formed in Brooklyn in 1967; Hough Area Development Corporation in Cleveland, OH organized in 1968; and United Durham, Inc. in Durham, NC, founded in 1968. The formation of CDCs picked up momentum in the next few years. There were an estimated 64 CDCs in 1973, some supported by the Ford Foundation, some by federal anti-poverty programs and some by both. This number mushroomed to about 1,000 in 1980. The National Congress for Community Economic Development estimates that there were about 2,200 CDCs in 1995. It's noteworthy that, despite the termination of special federal funding for CDCs in the late 1970s, about three-quarters of the CDCs receiving federal assistance in the late 1960s and early 1970s were still in operation in 1996. Whatever the exact number today, there's no question that a small experiment in a few devastated urban black neighborhoods has now become an established means to carry out locally responsive development in all parts of the United States – in urban and rural areas; and in black, white, Hispanic, Asian, Native American and ethnically mixed communities.

Some CDCs, such as Common Wealth, Inc., serve small neighborhoods. Common Wealth is located in the Williamson-Marquette neighborhood, with a population of about 3,000, in Madison, WI. In contrast, Bedford Stuyvesant Restoration Corporation's impact area has more than 400,000 people. Alaska Village Initiatives serves 200 villages of indigenous people scattered throughout the state. Kentucky Highlands is located in nine poor Appalachian counties in southeastern Kentucky.

What these diverse organizations have in common is a model of community and economic development in which local people identify their most important needs and, working through the CDC, find solutions to meet those needs. While CDCs are organized as non-profit corporations rather than as cooperatives, they have many cooperative features. Their mission is to serve a community of members and, in most cases, the members elect the board of directors to oversee this mission. In fact, the National Cooperative Bank, which provides financial assistance to consumer and employee-owned cooperatives, treats CDCs as part of the co-op family. Following are a few examples of how this model works in action.

DESIGNING SOCIAL CHANGE BY THE BAY

A group of Asian-American architectural students from the University of California-Berkeley launched Asian Neighborhood Design (AND) in 1973. They wanted to apply the benefits of their training to development projects in Chinatown and other Asian neighborhoods of the San Francisco Bay area. By late 1995, AND had evolved into a large, multicultural and highly respected community development corporation with a $4 million budget and more than 60 staff members. In addition to the original architecture and planning services, AND's work gradually has expanded to include business development; community resources and education; employment training; housing; and community development. Likewise, its clientele has grown to include African-Americans, Hispanics and whites. In 1995, only about one-third of AND's clients were Asians and Asian-Americans.

One of AND's major accomplishments has been to develop an employment training program for high-risk youth. A small, hands-on training program begun in 1978 is now Specialty Mill Products, a profitable furniture manufacturing subsidiary with a gross annual income of $1.5 million and more than 30 employees in 1995. The company's beds, cabinets and other furniture are designed for small, low-income housing units, although their attractive, practical and sturdy construction appeals to a much broader customer base. The success of Specialty Mill Products epitomizes AND's integrated philosophy and practice. Through Specialty Mill, AND addresses low-income housing needs, provides a training program and jobs for youth, and operates a profit center that helps to support the whole organization. In 1995, AND opened a second Specialty Mill Products manufacturing site in Oakland and is planning to open a third plant in Boston in 1996, working cooperatively with Dudley Square Neighborhood Initiative, a community-based organization.

AND's commitment to youth employment training extends beyond its furniture subsidiary. The organization has established the Employment Training Center, a school licensed by the state of California, to provide both general education and job training to dropouts and other young people who aren't making it in school or in the labor market. In 1995, more than 120 trainees were enrolled in the center's intensive cabinet-making and construction trades training program. More than 75 percent of the center's trainees successfully complete the program. As one graduate put it, "[The training program] made me feel better about myself, because I was actually accomplishing something.... If it hadn't been for the training program, I'd either be selling drugs, dead, or in jail."

For an organization that started out in architectural design, AND's strong expansion into human development areas is an impressive accomplishment. It helps low-income individuals and families to develop skills and become self-sufficient. For example, the CDC has developed a 38-unit intergenerational apartment complex in partnership with San Francisco Network Ministries that is not just a place to live, but also a "life center for the working poor." Residents work together on their academic and job skills, have access to counseling, and learn how to cope better with family stresses and strains. There's even rooftop garden space where each resident can grow flowers or vegetables. All together in 1995, AND provided counseling and housing support services to 1,700 low-income tenants.

Being a community-based design center continues to be one of AND's most important activities. In 1995, the organization provided architectural, design and real estate development services to 60 community-based organizations. These services were targeted to projects serving low-income people and to neighborhood revitalization programs.

Asian Neighborhood Design represents a highly creative, multifaceted approach to helping people become economically and socially self-sufficient and to helping depressed neighborhoods regain a feeling of community. The work of a few architectural students with vision has evolved into a community development corporation that has improved community life throughout the Bay area and, by example, far beyond.

CASTING A WIDE NET IN MAINE

Coastal Enterprises, Inc. (CEI), headquartered in Portland, defines the entire state of Maine as its impact area. As its name implies, CEI once had a narrower focus. This CDC started in 1977 with the mission of improving the economic condition of Maine's coastal fishing communities. To this end, CEI developed fishing cooperatives, set up a processing plant, organized a fishery-related employment training program and established an export company.

After five years of successful fishery development work, the organization branched out in new directions. Now CEI defines its role as a financial and technical assistance intermediary. This is a fancy way of saying that the CDC uses its limited resources to help make a lot of things happen. For example, it has a loan program for small Maine manufacturers and other businesses. The financing terms are good, but they come with a catch. Part of the package is that employers agree to hire low-income and disabled workers.

CEI also helps community groups organize affordable housing programs and, in some cases, plays the role of low-income housing developer. The CDC also runs one of Maine's Small Business Development Centers – the most productive one in the state.

Coastal Development Services is CEI's newest venture. Its mission is to assist other community-based groups in the United States and abroad – especially in central and eastern Europe – to carry out successful business and housing projects that meet the needs of local residents. Ron Phillips, CEI's executive director, is of Albanian descent and has made several consulting trips to Albania and other central European states to promote locally based approaches to development.

CEI's diversified development strategy has been critical to its survival and growth over the past 15 years. The fisheries of New England and the Canadian Maritime Provinces have experienced depressed conditions in the early and mid-1990s, primarily due to overfishing. In the last half of the 1970s, CEI helped small-scale fishermen compete more effectively through co-ops, joint processing and joint marketing. Recently the organization's role has been to work with these fishermen and their communities to become less dependent on fishing and to diversify their local economies into manufacturing and tourist-related businesses.

REVIVAL IN NEWARK

Newark, NJ did not escape the racial turmoil and civil disorders of the 1960s. In July 1967, allegations of police brutality toward a black cab driver escalated into a riot that left 23 people dead, 1,020 injured and $15 million in property damage in Newark's Central Ward. Six months later, New Community Corporation rose almost literally out of the ashes. Under the leadership of Father (now Msgr.) William Linder, the pastor of an inner-city parish, and a group of religious and lay leaders, this new organization was formed to make a constructive response to the unrest in the Central Ward and the underlying community problems. New Community was intended to be a comprehensive service organization addressing the social and economic problems that plagued the 50,000 predominantly black residents of the Central Ward.

New Community represents a partnership among neighborhood residents, who have eight of nine seats on the board; religious congregations from Newark and its suburbs; and city and state officials. In the past 28 years, this unique cooperative effort has produced a large, complex CDC with 37 affiliate organizations providing a range of social services – from child care to home-care services for the elderly; housing construction and management services; real estate services; ownership of a neighborhood shopping center; employment and training services; and individual and small business financial services. Following are a few examples of New Community's activities.

• **Housing.** In 1996, the city of Newark is razing 288 units of poorly constructed, unpopular public housing. On the same site New Community will be using a grant from the Department of Housing and Urban Development to build 206 townhouses providing home ownership opportunities to low- and extremely low-income Central Ward residents. If successful, this project will provide a national model of how to replace the demeaning living conditions of many public housing projects with attractive housing units owned and maintained by the residents.

New Community also owns and manages 3,100 units of rental housing for seniors, families and others.

• **Services.** The CDC provides a broad array of services to virtually every age group, including seven day care centers serving more than 700 children, home health-care services and a number of youth programs.

• **Economic Development.** New Community and its affiliates employ 1,400 people. Many work in the CDC-owned neighborhood shopping center, which has a supermarket and more than eight other businesses owned by New Community.

• **Employment and Training.** The CDC operates a full-service employment and training center that places about 1,000 people in jobs each year. The center also has a GED training program providing high school dropouts with the opportunity to get the equivalent of a high school diploma. Several hundred job seekers participate in this program each year.

• **Financial Services.** New Community has organized a credit union with 2,300 members. In early 1996, the credit union applied for a grant under the federal Community Development Finance Institution program. This grant would assist the credit union to provide a range of services to local residents and businesses including low-cost home buyer mortgages and a micro-business loan fund. The CDC also has organized a multibank development loan fund, in which seven Newark area banks have committed $400,000 per year to business development projects in New Community's service area.

These examples illustrate some of the diverse ways New Community is building a new community in Newark's Central Ward. The word that characterizes this CDC's approach to development better than any other is "comprehensive." Whether the need has been social, housing or economic development, New Community has established a program to meet that need during its productive 28-year history.

TRADING UP IN NAVAHO

One of the images from the bad old days of white-Indian relations is of traders ripping off Native Americans when they came to purchase and barter goods at trading posts. That image is not as far back in time as we might like it to be. In the late 1960s, residents of Pinon, AZ, on the Navaho reservation, brought a class action suit against the local trader, who ran the only general goods store in town. They also formed a cooperatively owned store to provide an alternative shopping place to the trading post.

The Pinon idea caught on in other reservation communities. Other groups formed a half dozen or so local co-ops in areas where people were dissatisfied with non-Indian traders. During the 1970s, managers or other local residents bought out these cooperatives; some others went under. Three or four of these stores were still in operation in 1996.

Taking on the traders and providing locally owned alternative stores is only the beginning of the story. This successful initial foray into economic self-determination led to the formation of Dineh Cooperatives, Inc. (DCI), a community development corporation that has created more than 850 permanent jobs on the reservation, has two profitable subsidiaries (a shopping center and a manufacturing company), and has also carried out ambitious hospital and housing projects.

Dineh is the Navaho word for "the people," and DCI is a people's organization. Community residents elect 14 board members who appoint two additional directors. The board makes the policy decisions for this multimillion dollar organization. DCI's primary impact area is the central and southwestern part of the reservation. The area has a population of about 25,000. The organization's broader goal is to serve all 135,000 Navahos on the reservation, which has an unemployment rate around 50 percent.

The DCI Shopping Center is a wholly owned subsidiary of DCI, located in Chinle, AZ, near the center of the reservation. The shopping center was initiated in the 1970s and was DCI's first large-scale project. One of the difficulties of doing economic development projects on reservation land is securing a long-term lease, since the sale of Navaho land is prohibited. According to Jon Colvin, the CEO of Dineh Cooperatives, it takes from six to 10 years to secure a long-term lease. DCI's perseverance paid off in the case of the shopping center. As of 1995, 15 stores subleased all the available square footage from DCI; they employed 180 people and generated sales of $16 million. In 1996, DCI was in the process of expanding the mall for the fifth time and was planning a sixth expansion for 1997. The significance of the shopping center is that it dramatically overturns the old trading-post pattern of outside ownership and the exporting of capital off the reservation. Colvin states DCI's intent very clearly: "We are attempting to change a colonial economy into an equal financial and trade partner with the rest of America by creating an active and viable private sector in the Navaho Nation."

Tooh Dineh Industries represents the second bold economic development project of DCI. It, too, is a wholly owned subsidiary. It began in 1983 as a three-person precision machinist shop in Leupp, AZ, in the southwest corner of the reservation. By 1995, Tooh Dineh had become an electronics manufacturing firm with about $50 million in annual sales and 400 employees.

DCI received outside support in the development of these two businesses, especially from the Community Services Administration and the block grant program of the U.S. Department of Housing and Urban Development. DCI still seeks out grant and loan funds for its new development projects, but now that its two major ventures are up and running successfully, the organization's profits support its core operations.

In addition to its entrepreneurial activities, DCI also plays the role of catalyst on the reservation. Several examples include: the lead organizing, planning and grant-writing role in the development of a $32 million comprehensive health-care facility in the late 1970s; assistance in the development of the Chinle Community Fire Department; and efforts in 1996 to develop on-reservation options for middle-income housing – a problem complicated by the tribe's leasing limitations. These community development efforts, as impressive as they are, are a sidelight to DCI's primary mission of creating businesses and jobs on the reservation.

In the long term, Dineh Cooperatives, Inc. wants to replicate its business development success throughout Navaho country, helping to form small and medium-size businesses that establish "an active and viable private sector in the Navaho Nation," far removed from the trading-post economy that dominated the reservation less than three decades ago.

VILLAGE ENTREPRENEURS IN ALASKA

It's hard to imagine a community development organization that operates in a 571,000-square-mile area, a territory that is more than one-seventh the size of the United States. Alaska Village Initiatives (AVI) has been facing this challenge since its formation in 1968. Fortunately, it doesn't serve every square mile of that area, but the 200 Alaska native villages that it does serve are scattered throughout the largest and least densely populated state in the Union.

Originally created under the name Community Enterprise Development Corporation of Alaska, Alaska Village Initiatives was rechristened in 1993 in part to reflect a shift in its mission toward greater emphasis on village-level business development. AVI has similar historical experiences to both Coastal Enterprises and Dineh Cooperatives. Like Coastal Enterprises, AVI was heavily involved in the fishing industry in its early years, organizing several fishing cooperatives and acquiring partial ownership in a salmon processing plant. Like Dineh Cooperatives, AVI assisted villagers to form consumer cooperatives – 10 in 1969 and 1970 alone – as an alternative to the Alaska Commercial Company stores, the equivalent of the trading posts on the Navaho reservation.

Also similar to these other two CDCs, AVI has shifted priorities since the early days. By 1992, the fishing industry in much of Alaska, as in Maine, had fallen on hard times. AVI's fishery development efforts were scaled down accordingly. Some of the village consumer cooperatives are still operating. However, AVI decided that the best way to compete with the "trading posts" was to own them. The CDC purchased the Alaska Commercial Company in 1977. By 1993, AVI had modernized its 23 village stores and turned the company into a successful business with $62 million per year in sales and 500 employees. At that time, it was the ninth largest Alaska-based employer.

In 1992 and 1993, AVI underwent a major change in its development philosophy and strategy. The board and staff decided the organization would have the most positive impact on the communities it served by being financially self-sufficient in its operations and by concentrating on financial assistance, technical assistance and demonstration projects. Running a major business such as the Alaska Commercial Company took too much time away from these objectives. Accordingly, AVI sold the company to a Canadian buyer who the board felt confident would provide continued high-quality management of the stores and would invest new capital in them.

As of early 1996, AVI was primarily in the business of micro-enterprise assistance in the form of training sessions, consulting and loans. One of the ironies of the organization's recent change in priorities is that business services that AVI used to provide for free or with a subsidy are now offered at market-rate or close to market-rate – and the popularity of these services is greater than ever. For example, AVI's spring 1996 rural small business conference was sold out, with 250 participants willing to pay $150 each for an event that used to have a nominal charge.

Cottage industries and small tourism businesses are growth areas in native villages. One business in a village of a few dozen native Alaskans employs three people making buttons out of caribou antler. AVI also helped 12 small, locally owned tour companies form a marketing cooperative that mass-mails 100,000 brochures per year to prospective clients.

One area in which AVI continues to play the lead development and ownership role is light industry, as long as the project does not compete with already established businesses.

Like Coastal Enterprises, AVI also has recently begun to provide business consulting assistance abroad. International Initiatives, a newly formed subsidiary, is focusing initially on micro-enterprise development in Russia, a short flight across the Bering Sea.

The story of Alaska Village Initiatives is one of adapting to external economic conditions and also of taking stock internally. AVI appears to be making a successful transition from being a large business owner doing small-enterprise development on the side to being primarily a multiservice assistance provider to native Alaskan micro-entrepreneurs.

SHARING THE WEALTH IN MADISON

The Williamson-Marquette neighborhood in Madison, WI is vastly different from Native American villages in Alaska or Arizona, or from a central-city neighborhood in Newark. It's only about a mile long and a half-mile wide with a population of around 3,000. Most of the residents are white, but the neighborhood is home to black, Asian, and Hispanic families as well. It's not a poor neighborhood, nor is it run down, nor does it have a particularly high drug or crime rate. Yet Williamson-Marquette, which is not unlike thousands of urban, suburban and small-town neighborhoods in terms of its demographic characteristics, does have a community development corporation.

Common Wealth Development, Inc. (CW) has its origin in a protest against the location of a prefabricated, fast-food restaurant on Williamson Street in the late 1970s. An organized group of neighbors was able to steer the franchisee to another part of town (and to a less objectionable design). The proposed restaurant site became an attractive "vest pocket" park.

Not satisfied with a successful protest, a group of neighborhood leaders decided to focus on planning and carrying out positive projects. They knew what they didn't want; now the challenge was to figure out and implement what they did want. Common Wealth was formed in 1979 with a three-part mission: to improve the housing stock; to do business and job development; and to improve the neighborhood as a place to live.

This scrappy little organization has been carrying out its mission ever since. Following is a sampling of some of its projects:

• **Housing.** An early project was the renovation of the "four yellow houses." A local slumlord owned four adjacent houses on Williamson Street that had been cited for a long list of housing code violations, including peeling paint. The landlord's response was to paint the fronts of the houses (but not the sides or backs) a garish yellow color – hence their name. Common Wealth acquired the houses, did a major renovation and turned the buildings into an eight-unit housing cooperative with one handicapped-accessible apartment.

CW has done several other housing projects as well, including: an eight-unit low-income housing cooperative completed in 1991, with four units specifically designed for people with physical disabilities; an eight-unit apartment complex renovated in the late 1980s and designed as transitional housing for women and children who had been victims of domestic abuse; and a sweat-equity and low-cost mortgage program intended to help low- and very low-income people buy their own homes.

• **Business and Jobs.** CW's showcase business development project is the Madison Enterprise Center. The center currently houses 15 small businesses and seven artisan studios. CW provides below-market-rate space and a number of shared services for its tenants, including business consulting; reception services; use of computers, copying machines and other equipment; and marketing assistance. In return, tenants agree to give priority to hiring low- and moderate-income employees. More than 60 people work in the building that is leased for $1 per year from Madison Gas and Electric. In addition, at least four businesses had "graduated" from the center by late 1995 and relocated within the neighborhood retaining about 25 additional jobs.

Because the Madison Enterprise Center had a long waiting list in the early and middle 1990s and because its mission was to provide temporary tenancy to small new businesses, CW renovated an old

Greyhound terminal in the neighborhood to meet the demand for additional long-term business space. Main Street Industries opened in early 1996, with four businesses relocating from the center and thus opening up room for new ventures on the center's waiting list. In 1996, CW plans to have 18 or 19 businesses located in Main Street Industries. As with the center, tenants will agree to give priority in their hiring to low- and moderate-income employees.

CW also has developed and improved retail space along Williamson Street to strengthen the neighborhood as a place to shop as well as to live. Projects include a four-business mini-mall, an expansion of a grocery co-op and a bicycle shop.

• **Community Building.** CW has developed a youth business mentoring program in which at-risk neighborhood kids, aged 14 to 16, work in area businesses after school, with their wages paid by the mentoring program. The program has proved so popular with both the kids and the business people that CW has been asked to expand it into other neighborhoods. In 1996, CW staff expect to have 125 youths participating in the program in four neighborhoods.

The Willy Street Fair represents community building of a different kind. The fair is an annual September event bringing thousands of neighborhood residents and others together for a day of music, games, costumes and socializing. Common Wealth staff and volunteers take the lead role in planning and organizing this celebration of community.

What characterizes Common Wealth more than anything else is its resiliency, tenacity and ability to remain focused on its three-part mission over its 16-year history. As with other community development corporations, it has had to rely for financial support on a variety of funding sources, including private foundations and local, state and federal government programs. Changing public and private agendas have required new approaches. Throughout all this, Common Wealth has not only survived, but it also has continued to find ways to make Williamson-Marquette a better place in which to live, work, do business and have a sense of community.

COOPERATIVE COMMUNITY PLANNING

One possible reaction to the successful CDC examples cited above is: "That's too big or too complex for our neighborhood or community. Besides, we don't have the ability (or the desire) to go after that kind of grant or loan money." If this is your reaction, there's a variation of bottom-up community development that might appeal to you. In this model, community residents get together to carry out a cooperative planning process. Citizen planners identify problems in their community, prioritize them, identify possible solutions and develop plans for carrying them out. The citizen planners may choose to play an active role in implementing the ideas they come up with, or they may pass on that responsibility to local governments, local business organizations, the school board or some other group.

On the other hand, after going through a cooperative development planning process, a local citizen group may decide that the best way to carry out the plans they have developed is to form a new community-based organization. Following are some examples of cooperative planning at the local community level.

CULTIVATING RURAL ACTION IN IOWA

Something got lost in rural America about three decades ago: the realization that agricultural production and processing is the main economic activity in this country's rural counties. Instead, local and state governments, chambers of commerce and industrial development corporations went off prospecting for outside businesses to relocate to their communities, often providing lucrative enticements in the form of cheap land, low taxes and subsidized loans. All of this was in the name of "economic development."

In 1993, Iowa's Department of Economic Development rediscovered that farms and locally based agricultural processing are economic development, too. Department officials observed: "We don't have to chase around the country begging businesses to move to industrial parks in our rural areas. The farms are already there. The raw materials, in the form of agricultural products, are already there. The business investors – farmers and other local residents – are already there." The missing ingredient was local planning to turn these opportunities into economic benefits.

Rural Action! was the department's innovative program designed to reintroduce agriculture into the economic development repertoire of Iowa's rural counties. The department hired Cooperative Development Services of Madison, WI, to prepare a manual, facilitate the planning sessions and assist with project feasibility studies. The W.K. Kellogg Foundation provided some financial support for this effort and for similar ones in Minnesota and Wisconsin. In 1994 and 1995, eight Iowa counties were selected on a competitive basis to participate in the program. Each county had a local coordinator and a *Rural Action!* committee consisting of about 20 farmers, business people, local government representatives and other citizens from around the county. Using the planning manual, a professional facilitator led the committees through a cooperative planning process that involved five or six meetings over the course of a year.

- Committee members first identified the major agriculture-related problems that affected their county and prioritized them.
- They then identified possible projects that addressed the top priority problems and selected three or four potential projects for further action.
- At this point, the committee divided into three or four subcommittees corresponding to the potential projects and studied the feasibility of each proposed project. This analysis took place over a period of several months.
- At the end of the feasibility study phase, each committee determined whether its project was worth pursuing.
- For those projects that appeared feasible, the next step depended on the complexity and cost of the project. In some cases, the committee decided to move right into the implementation phase. In other cases, a more detailed business plan had to be prepared and financing had to be secured.

Following are a few examples of projects undertaken by some of the eight Iowa counties that participated in *Rural Action!* in 1994 and 1995.

IDENTITY PRESERVED GRAINS

Over half of the eight county planning groups selected "identity preserved grains" as one of their priority projects. The idea behind these projects is simple. Corn is not corn is not corn. There are different kinds of corn (and soybeans and wheat, etc.), some of which receive higher prices in the marketplace than others. For example, there is a high-oil corn that is a better animal feed. A low-fat soybean produces a healthier cooking oil. There are grains that are grown organically – without chemical fertilizers, herbicides and pesticides. All of these receive a premium price in the marketplace.

The trick is to link up farmers with buyers of these specialty grains and, in some cases, to provide assistance to producers who are trying out new seed varieties and farming practices. Some of the county groups helped farmers get contracts with established buyers, others linked them up with marketing co-ops, and one is working with farmers on forming a new specialty crop co-op.

MOBILE MANURE SEPARATOR

This may not sound like a glamorous project, but in a state like Iowa, with a large hog and cattle population, animal waste is a serious concern – and a golden-brown opportunity. The two big problems related to manure disposal in Iowa are water pollution and odor. A project identified by the Fayette County group was to create a new farmer-owned business in the county that would remove manure solids from area farms; compost the manure with recycled newsprint, yard waste and other waste materials; and bag and sell the resulting product as a high-quality compost. The project also addresses the smell issue – identified by Iowans as the number one agricultural problem in the state – because separating waste solids and liquids substantially reduces the odor from fermentation, and because well-regulated composting is virtually odor-free.

OTHER PROJECTS

Other *Rural Action!* projects included vacation farm tours; local, farmer-owned grain processing facilities; an ethanol plant (this county project joined forces with a larger regional project); several projects intended to get a higher return for local farmers on their livestock; an alfalfa marketing co-op; and a program to assist in the transfer of farms from retiring farmers to young farmers.

Rural Action! has proven to be an effective partnership between the state of Iowa and local citizens interested in building on the strengths of their agricultural resources. A wealth of local leadership, creative ideas and business development savvy has emerged in the eight county-level, cooperative development planning groups. This model has excellent potential for adaptation in thousands of other rural counties that want to rediscover the dynamic role agriculture can play in local economic development.

TOWNS NOT DOWN AND OUT IN WISCONSIN

The Wisconsin Towns Association sponsored three rural, county-based planning groups in 1995 that were similar to Iowa's, although they did not have an exclusively agricultural orientation. Cooperative Development Services, with financial support from the W.K. Kellogg Foundation, provided staffing for these groups. Despite the broader planning mission, all three groups selected at least one agricultural project for feasibility analysis. Other projects included services to recreational property owners, two tourism projects and a forestry cooperative. Probably the most innovative project was the Vernon County plan to strengthen the role of local artisans in the community and to increase their incomes by identifying new marketing opportunities and by building an area craft school.

The planning work in Wisconsin sponsored by the towns association illustrates the point that local cooperative development planning can be supported in a wide variety of ways. States can play a major role, as in Iowa. Local government units – counties, cities, villages and towns – can be the catalysts, either individually or jointly. Private entities – such as rural electric cooperatives, public utilities, chambers of commerce, neighborhood organizations, church groups and foundations – can all provide support for this kind of cooperative planning.

Even though the examples presented above are all in rural counties, this citizen-based planning is equally effective in urban neighborhoods. The critical needs are that, first, *somebody* get the ball rolling, and second, that the planning process be conducted in an efficient manner, combining a balance of active participant involvement and genuine movement toward the identification and implementation of achievable objectives.

CONCLUSION

The primary theme of this chapter is that community residents can make a difference in shaping the future of their neighborhoods, cities, villages and counties by cooperatively planning and carrying out projects. The chapter also has several subthemes:

1. There is no "right" population size or geographical area for local cooperative action. Small or large urban neighborhoods can do it. Organizations serving different-sized rural areas also can carry out successful cooperative projects.

2. Beyond planning and working cooperatively and using good social and economic judgment, there is no right way to do good community projects. In some of the examples described above, local planning groups have been catalysts and "nudgers" to get local governments or business groups moving. On the other end of the spectrum, some projects have evolved into large development organizations with hundreds of employees planning and implementing dozens of programs. Both approaches are good as long as they are accountable and responsive to community needs.

3. Starting off with manageable-sized projects is important. Despite the range of workable cooperative action models they have developed, all of the examples in this chapter have selected a geographical focus and have carried out an initial project or set of projects that they could handle.

4. The final subtheme is "do something." All of the above examples represent community groups taking action. It would have been tedious to present a sampling from the tens of thousands of communities around the country in which people perceive local problems and opportunities, but do nothing about them. Cooperative community action works, but only if local citizens make it work.

Finally, the underlying premise for community cooperation is articulated beautifully in the following quote from a January 1996 *U.S. News and World Report* article about the loss of social and civic involvement in contemporary America and the efforts that some communities are making to change this: "[T]he infrastructure of civic life remains intact, even in some of the nation's poorest neighborhoods. It's just waiting to be rediscovered."

ACKNOWLEDGMENTS
Kathy Beery, Iowa Department of Economic Development, Des Moines, IA.
Jon Colvin, Dineh Cooperatives, Inc., Chinle, AZ.
Perry Eaton, Alaska Village Initiatives, Anchorage, Alaska.
Sue Lambertz, Iowa Department of Economic Development, Des Moines, IA.
Jenifer Logan, Coastal Enterprises, Inc., Portland, ME.
Maurice Miller, Asian Neighborhood Design, San Francisco, CA
Maryianne Morton, Common Wealth Development, Inc., Madison, WI
Rona Parker, New Community Corporation, Newark, NJ.
Terry Simonette, National Cooperative Bank Development Corporation, Washington, D.C.
Bob Zdenek, New Community Corporation, Newark, NJ; formerly with the National Congress for Community Economic Development, Washington, D.C.

REFERENCES
Cooperative Development Services. 1994. **Rural Development Powerbook**. Madison, WI: Cooperative Development Services. *(The cooperative development manual used for community planning in Iowa, Minnesota and Wisconsin.)*

Faux, Geoffrey. 1971. **CDCs: New Hope for the Inner City.** New York: The Twentieth Century Fund. *(A good account of the early days of CDCs and the strategy behind them.)*

Ford Foundation. 1973. **Community Development Corporations: A Strategy for Depressed Urban and Rural Areas**. New York: Ford Foundation.

Harrison, Bennett. 1995. **Building Bridges: Community Development Corporations and the World of Employment Training**. New York: Ford Foundation.

McKnight, John. 1995. **The Careless Society: Community and Its Counterfeits.** New York : BasicBooks.

Peirce, Neil R. and Steinbach, Carol F. 1987. **Corrective Capitalism : The Rising Tide of America's Community Development Corporations.** New York : Ford Foundation.

Perry, Stewart E. 1987. **Communities on the Way : Rebuilding Local Economies in the United States and Canada**. Albany: State Univ. of New York Press.

Ritchie, Barbara. 1969. **The Riot Report.** New York: Viking Press.

CHAPTER 12.

LOCAL GOVERNMENTS:
FORGING PARTNERSHIPS & LEAVING OLD RIVALRIES BEHIND

Towns, villages, cities, counties and school districts face a variety of political and economic pressures causing them to search for ways to cut costs, improve services or add new ones – sometimes all at the same time. This chapter provides examples of how some communities have accomplished this seemingly impossible set of tasks through cooperative purchasing and sharing of services; the use of telecommunications to educate students at multiple sites; joint recycling services; and a state program that assists a range of cooperative activities at the local level.

NEIGHBORING COMMUNITIES: FRIENDS OR FOES?

The 15 towns and villages of Tioga County, NY, have learned to cooperate. In 1991, they saved their citizens $200,000 through a joint health insurance program. They also cut costs on highway and office supply purchases and simultaneously reduced the cost and improved the quality of safety training for municipal workers.

The state of Pennsylvania is promoting and assisting cooperation through its *Intergovernmental Cooperation Handbook.*

Twenty-three government agencies collaborated to form a transit authority in rural Sweetwater County, WY. The result of consolidated transportation services in a county the size of Vermont is more riders at no increase in cost.

Cities in metropolitan areas cooperate, too. Twenty-eight municipalities in the Milwaukee area have formed the Intergovernmental Cooperation Council. Members have jointly purchased police squad cars, collaborated on a household hazardous waste cleanup program, hired a telecomunications consultant and bid jointly on health insurance. Six communities have merged their fire departments. As one village president says: "... [I]t's better if we work together, instead of every community struggling along by itself."

These examples of local communities working together are the exception rather than the rule. The municipal equivalent of rugged individualism continues to impede joint action among local governments. Small and large communities alike tend to base their identities on a combination of local pride and antagonism toward their neighbors. One of the historical images of local communities and neighborhoods in America is a feudal one – a scattering of symbolically walled villages spread across both metropolitan areas and the countryside. The skirmishes among these fiefdoms have taken the form of high school sports rivalries, main street business competition and coffee shop gossip.

This feudal image still applies in many cities and towns, but it's beginning to be displaced by a far more collaborative one. Joint economic, social and educational projects are becoming increasingly common among neighboring communities. Sometimes this cooperation is informal – for example, providing ambulance services across jurisdictional lines. Sometimes it takes the form of a service contract, such as a city picking up garbage for a fee in a nearby unincorporated town. In some cases several nearby municipalities may enter into a joint powers agreement in which they carry out an activity as a group, such as recycling waste or buying school supplies. Regional councils, also known as councils of government, represent a fourth kind of local government cooperation. These councils are often multicounty bodies that carry out coordinated planning and review projects that may have an impact on their regions. Most states also have cooperative educational service agencies or agencies with similar names that provide cooperative sharing of services among school districts in sub-state regions.

There is no reliable estimate on the extent of local governmental cooperation in the United States. If informal cooperation is included, there may be thousands of examples. In this chapter, however, we will focus on a narrower range of projects involving shared purchasing, services and marketing by formally organized groups of more than two units of local government. We will exclude regional councils and cooperative educational service agencies from this discussion because these organizations are already well-established and researched. Based on this narrower criteria, we estimate there are 500 to 1, 000 examples of this kind of local government cooperation in the United States. This phenomenon appears to have grown dramatically in the 1980s and early 1990s. Given that there are about 85,000 units of local government in this country, it's clear that this kind of intercommunity cooperation is in its infancy.

Why are there an increasing number of local governments coming together to buy supplies jointly, share equipment and personnel, and, in general, stretch the value of local taxpayers' dollars? This incipient movement toward greater local cooperation is occurring for a variety of reasons. In some communities a decrease in the population has eroded the local tax base. In others, an increase in population has put pressure on sewer, water, street and school costs. High unemployment and business closures have been motivating factors for looking at joint solutions in some counties and regions. A reduction in state and federal resources has been a factor for many local governments. An irate local citizenry complaining about high taxes has been yet another.

Recent research and the school of hard knocks have dispelled many misconceptions about local and regional economic development strategies in the 1970s, '80s and '90s. As local governments have become disillusioned with unsuccessful strategies, they have become more willing to look to their neighbors for cooperative approaches. Information about how regional development works and doesn't work provides strong support for local communities banding together to build on their combined strengths. Joint approaches clearly beat competing against one another using development strategies with low odds for success.

One of the myths is that if a community builds an industrial park, industry will come. Unlike *Field of Dreams,* this economic development strategy usually doesn't work. Numerous cornfields with sewer and water hookups and abandoned urban warehouse districts that look like war zones attest to this sad fact. A growing body of research over the past two decades indicates that most local communities find that seeking jobs and economic growth through recruiting outside businesses doesn't pay off. Even those communities that do win this industrial lottery sometimes find out that they've given more in financial incentives than they get back in tax revenues and jobs. Or they find that the businesses they so arduously wooed are off to greener, sometimes foreign pastures, or close down after they have taken advantage of the incentives.

On the other hand, homegrown strategies for economic development – based on the expansion of already existing local businesses and the startup of new businesses by local entrepreneurs – generally have proven far more effective than "smokestack chasing" in generating job growth and in providing a good return on investment to the communities involved. Because they're locally based, these companies are much less likely to be footloose than businesses recruited from the outside.

Recent research also shows that the benefits of successful local economic development in one community extend to other communities within commuting distance. Direct and indirect job benefits are spread throughout this broader area. People shop, build homes and pay taxes not just in one community, but in many.

Effective regional economic development isn't the only benefit of local government cooperation. Quantity, quality, timeliness, stability, efficiency and economies of scale are all reasons cities, villages, towns, school districts and counties have joined together to purchase and share goods and services. Volume discounts apply to snowplows and fire engines as well as to toilet paper and erasers. Volume ordering also provides the ability to customize requests and to get orders met in a timely fashion. Shared services mean five communities making full use of an expensive piece of composting equipment rather than one community grossly underutilizing the equipment. In the same way, a cluster of villages can hire a full-time attorney or engineer rather than bringing in outside expertise that's far more expensive and not always available when needed.

As with other forms of cooperation, however, the success of intergovernmental collaboration is based on more than just good economic sense. The prerequisite is local officials who perceive the potential positive impact of mutual action and are willing to overcome local rivalries. Following are three examples of communities that have reaped the benefits of local government cooperation and one example of a state program that has fostered these joint efforts.

WACCO MAKES SENSE IN MINNESOTA

Laurie Mullen is the executive director of the Western Area Cities/Counties Cooperative (WACCO, pronounced whack-o) in Minnesota. Her previous job was as a buyer for a sporting goods store. She now coordinates equipment sharing, purchasing and joint workshops among 19 cities and nine counties in a mostly rural area of Minnesota. In the past two-and-a-half years, Mullen has played a lead role in transforming WACCO from a good idea to an effective organization.

"When I started in September 1993," Mullen says, "the city managers wanted the cooperative to begin working on many projects at once. I wanted to start out slowly and do a small number of things well." Her first initiative was to organize a series of meetings and picnics among the directors of public works departments in the member cities. Although they ran similar operations in neighboring communities, few of these department heads knew each other. The get-togethers organized by Mullen were a big success resulting in new friendships, information sharing, and, eventually, joint workshops and sharing of equipment among the public works departments.

"I don't tell people how to cooperate," she notes. "I ask them for ideas and recommendations. When they respond, I give them credit in our newsletter." Mullen also has done a series of surveys in the different departments of the member cities and counties to identify common needs and ideas for workshops and other services that WACCO might provide.

Mullen is particularly proud of the more than 80 workshops the cooperative organized for city and county personnel in 1993 and the first half of 1994. These workshops have saved WACCO members over $300,000 in fees and travel expenses. These savings come from the fact that workshops are held within the organization's nine-county service area. As a result, participants don't have to travel an average of 200 or more miles to the Minneapolis-St. Paul area and pay for meals and lodging while they're there. Workshop savings alone represent well over three times the current annual budget of this intergovernmental cooperative. The workshops have covered a wide range of topics including road maintenance, defensive driving, health and safety, specialized police officer training and employee rights.

The cooperative has its origins in a successful, informal equipment-sharing program developed by the cities of Fergus Falls and Perham, MN. The two city managers figured if this approach could work well for two cities, it could have an even bigger impact on saving money and improving services if more cities were involved. The fact that Fergus Falls also had an agreement with the neighboring town of Morris for jointly employing a building inspector provided a further impetus to expand intergovernmental cooperation in the region.

Representatives from 11 western Minnesota cities, ranging in size from Moorhead (30,000) to a number of communities with populations of a few hundred, met several times in 1991 and 1992 to discuss the idea of greater intercity cooperation. In early 1993, with the help of the Educational Cooperative Service Unit – a cooperative of school districts serving the region and based in Fergus Falls – the city managers submitted a grant request to Minnesota's West Central Initiative Fund to establish WACCO. The Initiative Fund approved the grant in the summer of 1993. The cities formed the cooperative under Minnesota's joint powers agreement statute and hired Mullen as executive director.

After her initial success with joint planning among public works department heads, Mullen organized similar get-togethers and planning sessions with fire chiefs, police chiefs and other municipal department heads. As a result of this "bottom-up" approach, most of the ideas implemented by WACCO for information and equipment sharing and joint training have come from local government personnel who know what their needs are. The more than 80 workshops organized by WACCO in less than a year-and-a-half attest to the effectiveness of this strategy.

WACCO grew rapidly in its first two years. Six additional cities joined the organization by the summer of 1994. Two more cities and all nine counties in which the member cities are located joined in the summer of 1995. All together, there were 28 local government members of the organization by the fall of 1995.

The next big push for WACCO will be to implement a computerized system for scheduling the sharing of personnel and equipment among member governments and for coordinating the purchasing of supplies and equipment. The co-op already is carrying out limited coordination of equipment sharing and supply purchasing. However, computer networking will speed up and expand the process and will greatly increase financial savings resulting from the cooperative.

For example, a city might post a notice on the computer network that it would like to rent a piece of composting equipment. Another city with the equipment would respond, and the two would negotiate a deal. Or, if several cities want to rent the same piece of specialized equipment, they may be able to save money by renting the equipment together. In fact, a group of WACCO member cities already have jointly leased a large tree grinder and a mobile piece of equipment called a "scarab," which chops and treats leaves and brush and rapidly accelerates their processing into reusable compost. In both these cases, joint leasing was far more cost-effective than leasing by individual cities.

The same type of approach can be used for purchasing. A county public works department may post a computer notice that it wants to buy four snowplow blades of a specific type. Other counties and cities can then add their own requests to the order. In most cases, WACCO will be able to get better prices on large-volume orders than the local governments would be able to get themselves on smaller orders.

At a time when most local governments are looking for innovative ways to contain costs without gutting local services, the kind of intergovernmental coordination exemplified by WACCO deserves close scrutiny. These 28 local governments are showing that cooperation can result in lower costs, improved training programs and other services, and a positive regional identity that goes beyond dollars and cents.

Overall, Mullen sums up her development strategy as follows: "Cooperation needs to start at the bottom. It can't be forced. What has made WACCO gain acceptance by department heads and other local government employees is that they feel they have nothing to lose by participating and an awful lot to gain." One measure of Mullen's and WACCO's success is that in June 1995 the organization won the City Achievement Award from the League of Minnesota Cities.

High school hockey rivalries in western Minnesota may still bring the partisans out to the rink on frigid Friday nights, but cooperatively purchased snowplow blades now clear the roads that get them there.

LEARNING TO COOPERATE AND COOPERATING TO LEARN IN WISCONSIN

Trempealeau County in western Wisconsin borders on the Mississippi River. Small dairy farms, wooded areas and villages divide up the landscape. The region's bluffs and rolling hills impart a bucolic beauty to the countryside, but also exact a price from those who choose to make a living from the land. The county's population is about 26,000. Arcadia, the largest city, has 2,200 residents. As with many agricultural areas in the United States, Trempealeau County has experienced a loss of farms (10 percent in the 1980s alone), a loss of farm-related jobs and, consequently, a loss of population in recent decades. These losses have been eased somewhat by growth in light industry, particularly by the presence of a large furniture manufacturer. Nonetheless, the small, dispersed population, coupled with the declining number of residents, has created problems for the county's economy and service sector. Educational services have not been immune from these problems.

A group of community leaders and school administrators began meeting in 1973 to address part of this overall problem. They were particularly concerned about the quality of education and the desire to minimize school consolidations. They believed that interactive television (often referred to as distance education) linking up the county's eight high schools would provide a way to increase the diversity of course offerings and reduce the need for school consolidations. They also recognized a broader community need that could be addressed at the same time: access to television services by the county's residents. The county had poor-quality reception because of the distance from television transmitters and the hilliness of the region and because cable companies considered it to be uneconomical to serve this low-density area.

The steering group incorporated the Western Wisconsin Communications Cooperative in 1975. The eight school districts in the county also entered into a cooperative agreement to form Project Circuit, a coordinating organization responsible for raising funds and bringing interactive cable programming into the schools. With the help of a W. K. Kellogg Foundation grant and loans from the Farmers Home Administration and the Rural Electrification Administration, these two organizations were able to start up cable services to the schools and county residents in 1979.

The origins of interschool cooperation go back well before the start of interactive cable programming. The Trempealeau Valley Cooperative, a project of four school districts established to coordinate educational services and busing, set the stage for Project Circuit and the Western Wisconsin Communications Cooperative in 1967. At that time, new federal and state mandates initiated educational programming requirements for students with special needs. The four school districts decided to share resources among themselves as a means to respond to these mandates. The districts were close enough together so that busing of students was an effective way to meet special educational needs in a cost-effective manner. In fact, this cooperative approach was so successful that the four schools expanded it to include vocational programming and college-bound courses.

For example, none of the schools had enough students for a third-year German class, but by bringing together students from several schools, they were able to offer the class. In the case of vocational training, relatively expensive equipment is required for such courses as woodworking, metal working, construction and automobile repair. By having one school specialize in each of these four areas of training, the schools could afford to meet these vocational training needs with professional instructors and quality equipment and facilities.

When the Western Wisconsin Communications Cooperative began operation in 1979, most of the college-bound classes, such as language, math and science courses, became part of the interactive cable curriculum and were no longer provided through Trempealeau Valley Cooperative's busing program. There also has been an increased emphasis in the 1980s and '90s to integrate students with special needs into "mainstream" classes. Thus, Trempealeau Valley Cooperative's primary focus in the mid-1990s is on vocational courses that require hands-on experience and specialized equipment and for which distance learning isn't feasible.

Sixteen years after Western Wisconsin Communications Cooperative and Project Circuit began operation, they're both still growing strong. The cooperative has about 6,500 cable subscribers. Project Circuit continues to be governed by eight school superintendents and has a multiyear lease agreement with the cooperative for interactive cable services. In fact, in 1996 the two organizations are developing a plan for an ambitious expansion of distance learning and other telecommunications services.

In 1996, one program with up to four sites (usually classrooms) can be hooked up at the same time. For example, a calculus teacher can have a class with three students at his or her site and small groups of students at three other sites. The people at all four sites can see each other on television monitors and talk to each other at the same time. One part of the plan would expand the capacity of the system to have two such programs occurring simultaneously.

Another part of the plan would make access to the Internet available through the cable network. One of the problems with Internet access in rural areas is that a long-distance call usually is required to get into the system. With multiple users, long-distance charges can get expensive fast. In Trempealeau County, the communications cooperative and the local telephone cooperative are developing a system that would allow the schools to communicate with one another and with the Internet at greatly reduced cost, thus opening up this immense, new educational medium to area students and faculty.

Schools, whether rural or urban, have tremendous opportunities to share resources with one another and to gain access to things they couldn't get on their own. In some cases such joint activities translate into lower costs; in other cases, into better learning experiences. Trempealeau county provides an excellent example of a case in which the quality and the cost-effectiveness of education are improving at the same time.

WASTING NOT IN NEW ENGLAND

As environmental awareness increased in the late 1970s and early 1980s and as landfill costs began to skyrocket, local governments in the densely populated northeast United States felt especially strong pressure to break out of old waste disposal patterns. A group of four municipalities formed the New Hampshire Resource Recovery Association in 1981 to provide a cooperative solution to their waste management problems.

The non-profit association started out with a joint newspaper marketing effort. Each town was too small to collect enough paper to interest a buyer. As a group, however, they were able to enter into a marketing agreement. Since this initial contract, the association, now known as the Northeast Resource Recovery Association (NRRA), has grown to about 200 voting municipal members in New Hampshire, Maine, Massachusetts and Vermont and a comparable number of nonvoting for-profit, non-profit and individual members. One measure of NRRA's success is that 50 recycling organizations in the United States and Canada have adopted the organization's resource-recovery model.

NRRA has seven different cooperative marketing programs (paper, plastics, aluminum and steel cans, scrap metal, glass containers, scrap tires and household textiles) and three purchasing cooperative programs (waste management supplies such as baling wire and recycling bags; pickup and disposal of household hazardous waste; and sorting mixed recyclables).

The essentials of the NRRA's marketing system are straightforward. On behalf of its members, the association puts out requests to buyers for bids on specific kinds of recyclables. A committee of members oversees each area of recyclables and selects the bid that most closely approximates the members' needs and preferences. Member municipalities are not bound to market their recyclables through the association, nor are buyers required to pay a prescribed price for them. Rather, the payment price for the recyclables fluctuates with the market. Buyers do agree, however, to purchase whatever volume of recyclables is made available by association members. This system works because municipalities are guaranteed a market for their recyclables based on the bargaining power of the association. The buyers, in turn, are able to get large quantities of materials that meet their quality requirements.

The value of the association to its members goes far beyond the negotiation and monitoring of these contracts. When small municipalities first get involved in recycling, they generally know little about how to collect and sort materials. The association provides the necessary training. After 14 years of operation, there are now about 200 small communities in New England with staff and volunteers who are recycling experts. Since recycling is a rapidly changing business, NRRA continues to play the lead role in communicating to its members and associate members changes in recycling laws and regulations, technology and markets.

As Peg Boyles, NRRA market development manager, says, "Cooperative marketing of recyclables is a complex endeavor, but it works. It has created a powerful network of highly trained operators at the local level that would not be present in a privatized system. The commitment to marketing recyclables has spread to the general population of these communities. There are financial benefits, as well, because of the revenue from the recycling market and because of the local jobs created."

THE STATE OF LOCAL GOVERNMENT COOPERATION IN IOWA

Sue Lambertz heads up the Iowa Department of Economic Development's Government Services Sharing Program. The program provides seed money for groups of local governments to develop cooperative programs. In her previous job, Lambertz coordinated a 13-city collaborative project in the Altoona area of central Iowa that was funded by the program she now administers.

Lambertz estimates that the cities in the Altoona area saved $100,000 in direct costs in the first year of their project through reduced insurance expenses, joint purchasing of safety equipment, joint publication of a safety policy manual, and other shared services and purchases.

The Government Service Sharing Program provides initial planning assistance and, if the local governments come up with a good plan, two-year grants for funding of an intergovernmental services coordinator. The municipalities are required to provide at least 25 percent in matching funds during the two-year period and to have a plan for full self-funding of the project after that time. The program has been in operation for three years and has provided assistance to 20 intergovernmental projects.

Projects receiving assistance thus far have included joint safety programs, shared mental health care services, collaborative agreements on fire protection and law enforcement, purchasing of insurance (as in the Altoona area communities), multicommunity planning projects and sharing of personnel (such as engineers and city clerks).

From the perspectives of both her local and her statewide work, Lambertz notes the energizing effect of getting a group of people together from neighboring communities to solve common local problems. "The process taps into local creativity," she says. "One community's need often matches another's resource." For example, a small town happened to own a vacant building that provided an ideal storage solution to a neighboring city's overflowing records problems.

Iowans are finding that a little bit of state assistance can go a long way to helping communities get untracked from their go-it-alone mindsets. The results have been impressive in terms of dollars saved, services improved and good will across municipal boundaries.

CONCLUSION

Cooperation works for local governments. It isn't just for farmers or consumers. When local public officials are able to put aside their differences with nearby units of government, good things happen. On the previous pages we have looked at a variety of different kinds of local government cooperatives that make purchases together, share services, sell recyclable materials and use interactive telecommunications as an educational resource. What these varied examples have in common is a group of public officials who have decided that they can meet the needs of local citizens and taxpayers more effectively by joining forces than by charging off on their own.

Despite these successful examples and dozens more like them, communities in the United States have barely scratched the surface of the potential for local government cooperation. This approach to shared services could be a powerful resource for rejuvenating urban and rural areas alike; for stimulating creative local solutions to economic and social problems; and for reclaiming a central role for decision-making by local governments and citizens in their own communities.

Some changes appear necessary for local government cooperation to blossom in the United States. State and federal government officials may need to devolve more decision-making power down to the local level. Following the example of Iowa, Minnesota, Pennsylvania and a few other states, more state and federal programs should provide incentives and rewards for intergovernmental cooperation. Most important of all, local government officials and community residents will need to change their views about neighboring communities so that they're perceived primarily as friends rather than as foes.

With these changes, local cooperation could play a lead role in improving the quality of life in small, medium and large cities and in the countryside. Whether the issue is education, police and fire protection, business and job development, housing, or any number of other issues, collaborative strategies work far better than feudalism.

ACKNOWLEDGMENTS

Kathy Beery, Iowa Department of Economic Development, Des Moines, IA.

Peg Boyles, Northeast Resource Recovery Assoc., Concord, NH

Beverly Cigler, Public Policy and Administration, Penn State Harrisburg, Middleton, PA.

Jerry Freimark, School Superintendent and Project Circuit Board Member, Whitehall, WI

Sue Lambertz, Iowa Department of Economic Development, Des Moines, IA.

Laurie Mullen, Western Assoc. of Cities/Counties Cooperative, Fergus Falls, MN

Mark Schroeder, Western Wisconsin Communications Cooperative, Independence, WI

Bill Urban, Cooperative Educational Services Agency, Fennimore, WI

REFERENCES

Bailey, Joan. 1994. "Tioga County Council of Local Governments: 'Building a Chemistry of Trust.' " Local Government Program, Cornell Univ., March.

Corporation for Enterprise Development. 1993. **Rethinking Rural Development.** Washington D.C.: Corporation for Enterprise Development. *(Well-documented analysis of the need for regional and local rural development strategies.)*

Johnson, Cindy. 1992. "Sweetwater County: Formation of a Transit Authority," in Peter F. Korsching et al., **Multicommunity Collaboration: An Evolving Rural Revitalization Strategy**, pp. 217-220. Ames, IA: North Central Regional Center for Rural Development.

Kurtz, Thomas S. 1990. *Intergovernmental Cooperation Handbook.* Trenton, Penn.: Pennsylvania Department of Community Affairs.

Schweke, William et al. 1994. **Bidding for Business: Are Cities and States Selling Themselves Short?** Washington D.C.: Corporation for Enterprise Development. *(A well-researched review of the misuse of public incentives in local and state economic development strategies.)*

Stark, Nancy T. Forthcoming. **Harvesting Hometown Jobs: A Guide to Sustainable Communities.** Washington, D.C.: The National Assoc. of Towns and Townships. *(A practical guide with step-by-step advice on how to build local development on local strengths and resources rather than importing it from the outside.)*

Thome, David. 1994. "Suburbs Find It Pays to Cooperate," *Milwaukee Journal.* October 4: 1.

Walker, David. 1987. "Snow White and the Seventeen Dwarfs: From Metro Cooperation to Governance." *National Civic Review.* January-February: 14-28.

CONCLUSION

This book has presented examples of how cooperation works in 12 different areas of our society. We have shown how people and organizations have accomplished common ends through joining forces in a wide variety of ways. So, why isn't there more of this kind of joint action? This concluding chapter presents some strategic ideas for increasing the amount of cooperation in the United States as we approach the 21st century. First, let's review the reasons for cooperating.

1. People working in groups are generally far more effective at achieving their goals than people working in isolation.

2. Working in groups is usually energizing. It feels good to be part of a team.

3. In many cases, we can accomplish things working together that we cannot accomplish alone. Examples include joint purchasing, in which we are able to access goods and services at lower prices and/or of better quality by pooling our buying power. If we're trying to sell something, joint marketing often gets us access to buyers whom we would not be able to reach on our own. Selling jointly can make our marketing costs far lower by each of us not having to produce separate marketing materials and to make separate marketing contacts. Joint action can provide us with services that we would not otherwise have access to – for example, a child care center, a food buying club, a health- care co-op.

4. Most importantly, cooperation works!

Our proposed strategy for increasing cooperative action at the person-to-person level consists of the following five components.

1. **Think cooperatively.** Behind every example of cooperation in this book is an individual or a group of individuals with an idea. We can change the way we go through our day-to-day lives simply by making it a habit to pose the question: Can this activity be done more cooperatively?

A friend of one of the authors who has been an attorney for the past 20 years recently decided to apply his legal skills in a new way. Instead of defending clients in divorce proceedings or in labor-management disputes, he has decided to focus his energies on mediating these disputes. This represents a radical shift in the traditional role of an attorney. Instead of being a hired gun, this friend is becoming a conflict resolver. He sees his job now as helping to identify areas of cooperation and compromise, rather than fostering competition and conflict.

We all can identify opportunities for increasing cooperation in our workplaces, our communities and in our families – if we keep our eyes open.

2. **Believe that you can make a difference.** All too often, we let things happen rather than make things happen. A common theme in the examples given throughout this book is that groups of people decided to make something happen. They believed they could make a difference by acting together – and they did. Cooperative change has to involve the active involvement of everyday people. Unfortunately, too many people in our society are lulled into passive roles, believing that they can't do anything about what's going in their kids' schools, in their neighborhoods, and pretty much anywhere else. They decide that they're just along for the ride. This sense of impotence is a self-fulfilling prophecy. If we don't think we can change the world around us, we can't. If we do think we can change the world around us, we at least have a shot at it, especially if we join forces with other people in our attempt.

3. **Pick a specific issue on which to cooperate.** Cooperation is just an abstraction until we identify something to cooperate about. If we're going to make the world a more cooperative place, we need to do it one project at a time. Maybe there's something happening in your neighborhood that has become a bother to you and to others who live nearby. For example, a group of middle-school kids are hanging out when they should be in school, and you suspect them of some petty thievery and vandalism. Getting together with a group of neighbors to explore solutions to this problem is a cooperative activity, one which may lead to some constructive ideas about what to do with these budding juvenile delinquents. Perhaps the neighborhood meeting, in turn, might lead to a cooperatively oriented project between the neighborhood and the school, in which curricular and extracurricular changes are made to help these kids develop a greater sense of purpose (for example, Common Wealth's middle-school business mentoring program). This project may become a model for other neighborhoods and schools in your community. And so on.

4. **Plan carefully.** Whether it's a neighborhood project or a multimillion dollar pasta cooperative, participatory planning is of key importance. Thinking strategically and studying the potential outcomes of the cooperative project multiply the likelihood of success. A good strategic plan asks: What is our goal? Do we have a group of people

who are committed to working toward the accomplishment of this goal? Realistically, what are our chances of success? Can we mobilize the necessary resources – both time and money – to launch this project? What are the specific steps we need to take in order to carry it out? Over what period of time?

5. **Don't lose sight of the need for broad-based participation and support.** Historically, this has been one the shortcomings of established cooperatives. After the involvement and enthusiasm of the first generation of cooperative members, all too often the cooperative comes to be operated just like other organizations that are not owned and controlled by their members. It's easy to slide into this type of insulated decision-making by a small group of people, usually a management group and a board of directors, and to have only nominal involvement with the broader membership. It takes a lot of work to have broad-based, ongoing participation over the long term. It also takes creativity. And this takes us back to the first point: Think cooperatively. A number of examples presented in this book illustrate creative ways in which participatory democracy can work on an ongoing basis to get things done.

APPENDIX: THE 100 LARGEST COOPERATIVES IN THE U.S.A.

Compiled by the National Cooperative Bank
Revenue & Assests in Millions

	Cooperative	Revenue.	Assets	Industry		
1	Farmland Industries	6,678	1,926	Agric.	Kansas City	MO
2	Harvest State Cooperative	3,845	734	Agric.	St. Paul	MN
3	Wakefern Food Co-op.	3,741	616	SprMkt	Elizabeth	NJ
4	Land O'Lakes Inc.	2,859	943	Agric.	Arden Hills	MN
5	Associated Wholesale Grocers	2,611	332	SprMkt	Kansas City	MO
6	Associated Milk Producers	2,587	528	Agric.	San Antonio	TX
7	Cotter & Co. (True Value)	2,574	869	Hw/Lbr	Chicago	IL
8	Mid Am Dairymen	2,491	740	Agric.	Springfield(1)	MO
9	Roundy's Inc.	2,462	405	SprMkt	Pewaukee	WI
10	ACE Hardware Corp	2,326	725	Hw/Lbr	Hinsdale	IL
11	Spartan Stores	2,189	373	SprMkt	Grand Rapids	MI
12	Cenex	2,183	1,200	Agric.	St. Paul	MN
13	Countrymark Co-op, Inc.	2,039	506	Agric.	Indianapolis	IN
14	Certified Grocers of California Ltd.	1,874	401	SprMkt	Los Angelos	CA
15	ServiStar Corp.	1,735	505	Hw/Lbr	Butler	PA
16	Agway, Inc.	1,694	1,274	Agric.	Dewitt	NY
17	Hardware Wholesalers, Inc	1,564	405	Hw/Lbr	Ft. Wayne	IN
18	Gold Kist, Inc.	1,561	716	Agric.	Atlanta	GA
19	Lumberman's Merchandising Corp.	1,466	87	Hw/Lbr	Wayne	IN
20	Ag Processing, Inc.	1,377	504	Agric.	Omaha	NE
21	Ocean Spray	1,191	695	Agric.	Middleboro	MA
22	CF Industries, Inc.	1,182	1,113	Agric.	Lake Zurich	IL
23	Twin County Grocers	1,129	154	SprMkt	Edison	NJ
24	Agribank	1,129	15,646	$Fin	St. Paul(4)	MN
25	Associated Grocers	1,106	269	SprMkt	Seattle	WA
26	Healthpartners, Inc.	1,098	585	Health	Minneapolis(3)	MN
27	Oglethorpe Power Corp	1,065	6,418	Utility	Tucker	GA
28	U.S. Central Credit Union	1,036	18,680	$Fin	Shawnee Mission	KS
29	Group Health of Puget Sound	1,013	640	Health	Seattle	WA
30	Shurfine International`	994	37	SprMkt	Melrose Park	IL
31	Sunkist Growers, Inc.	967	229	Agric.	Van Nuys	CA
32	United Grocers	954	307	SprMkt	Portland	OR
33	S. States Cooperative	950	323	Agric.	Richmond	VA
34	Growmark, Inc.	884	439	Agric.	Bloomington	IL
35	Darigold Farms	878	906	Agric.	Seattle	WA
36	Co-Bank	937	13,863	$Fin	Denver	CO

37	Tri-Valley Growers	821	802	Agric.	San Francisco	CA
38	Associated Food Stores	809	170	SprMkt	Salt Lake City	UT
39	National Cooperative Refinery Assn.	797	211	Agric.	McPherson	KS
40	Plains Cotton Co-op Assn	797	211	Agric.	Lubbock	TX
41	Foremost Farms USA Co-op	779	188	Agric.	Baraboo(2)	WI
42	Calcot Ltd.	775	177	Agric.	Bakersfield	CA
43	California Milk Producers	774	110	Agric.	Artesia	CA
44	Prairie Farms Dairy, Inc.	772	242	Agric.	Carlinville	IL
45	Certified Grocers Midwest	699	132	SprMkt	Hodgkins	IL
46	Riceland Foods, Inc.	686	272	Agric.	Stuttgart	AR
47	Dairymen, Inc.	677	154	Agric.	Louisville(1)	KY
48	N. C. Electric Membership Copr.	672	1,542	Utility	Raleigh	NC
49	Dairyman's Co-op Creamery	637	125	Agric.	Tulare	CA
50	Associated Wholesalers, Inc.	619	83	SprMkt	Robesonia	PA
51	Navy Federal Credit Union	602	8,436	$Fin	Merrifield	VA
52	Atlantic Dairy Co-op	595	79	Agric.	Southampton	PA
53	Ag America Farm Credit Bank	569	7,242	$Fin	Spokane	WA
54	Western Corp. FCU	564	12,400	$Fin	San Dimas	CA
55	American Crystal Sugar	563	324	Agric.	Moorhead	MN
56	Calif. Almond Growers	562	159	Agric.	Sacramento	CA
57	Affiliated Foods	562	76	SprMkt	Amarillo	TX
58	Food Service Purchasing Cooperative	528	43	Franc.	Louisville	KY
59	MFA Incorporated	524	235	Agric.	Columbia	MO
60	MI Livestock Exchange	507	73	Agric.	E. Lansing	MI
61	California Gold Dairy Prod.	500	71	Agric.	Petaluma	CA
62	Associated Electric Co-op	486	1,487	Utility	Springfield	MO
63	Seminole Electric Co-op	481	994	Utility	Tampa	FL
64	Farm Credit Bank of Columbia	477	6,308	$Fin	Columbia(4)	SC
65	Affiliated Food Co-op	463	67	SprMkt	Norfolk	NE
66	Equity Co-op Livestock Sales	461	40	Agric.	Baraboo	WI
67	Staple Cotton Co-op Assn	453	67	Agric.	Greenwood	MS
68	URM Stores	447	114	SprMkt	Spokane	WA
69	Western Dairymen Co-op	443	88	Agric.	Denver	CO
70	Affiliated Foods Southwest	441	92	SprMkt	Little Rock	AR
71	SF Services, Inc.	439	160	Agric.	N. Little Rock	AR
72	Tri-State G&T Assn	438	1,290	Utility	Denver	CO
73	Recreational Equipment Inc	432	207	Recre.	Sumner	WA
74	Basin Electric Power Co-op	431	2,378	Utility	Bismarck	ND
75	Western Farm Credit Bank	430	5,239	$Fin	Sacramento(4)	CA
76	National Grape Co-op Assn	424	297	Agric.	Westfield	NY
77	Michigan Milk Producers	418	95	Agric.	Nori	MI
78	Agri-Mark, inc.	413	99	Agric.	Methuen	MA
79	Central Grocers Co-op	412	66	SprMkt	Franklin Park	IL
80	Dairylea Co-op, Inc.	409	44	Agric.	E. Syracuse	NY
81	Cajun Electric Power Co-op	380	2,136	Utility	Baton Rouge	LA
82	Piggly Wiggly Alabama	372	54	SprMkt	Bessemer	AL
83	Associated Press	371	221	Media	New York	NY
84	Md & Va Milk Producers, Inc.	363	57	Agric.	Reston	VA
85	Progressive Affiliated Lumbermen	356	28	Hw/Lbr	Grand Rapids	MI
86	Tennessee Farmers Co-op	352	99	Agric.	La Vergne	TN

87 Farm Credit Bank of Texas	340	4,273	$Fin	Austin(4)	TX
88 Old Dominion Electric Co-op	337	1,074	Utility	Richmond	VA
89 E. Kentucky Power Co-op	330	798	Utility	Winchester	KY
90 United Dairymen of AZ	325	36	Agric.	Tempe	AZ
91 CFC (NRUCFC)	325	6,224	$Fin	Herndon	VA
92 Milk Marketing Inc.	318	81	Agric.	Cleveland	OH
93 Allied Building Stores	317	22	Hw/Lbr	Monroe	LA
94 Big Rivers Electric Corp	316	1,132	Utility	Henderson	KY
95 Citrus World Inc.	308	176	Agric.	Lake Wales	FL
96 Associated Grocers	303	869	SprMkt	Baton Rouge	LA
97 Farm Credit Bank of Wichita	302	4,156	$Fin	Wichita(4)	KS
98 Central Electric Power Co-op	297	138	Utility	Columbia	SC
99 Corp. for Public Broadcasting	294	125	Media	Washington	DC
100 Arkansas Electric Co-op	293	810	Utility	Little Rock	AR
Total-In Millions	97,666	149,501			

(1) Dairymen, Inc. of Louisville merged with Mid-America Dairymen, Springfield, MO in September, 1994.

(2) Foremost Farms USA Cooperative is new name of Wisconsin Dairies Cooperative which merged with Golden Guernsey Cooperative, 1994.

(3) Healthpartners data are consolidated for all operations.

(4) Data revised in restructuring and consolidations within Farm Credit Banks.

INDEX

D

E

U

V

W

DAVID J. THOMPSON, an internationally known advisor to cooperatives, is President of Thompson Consulting. He has consulted for the United Nations and has major clients in the United States, Europe and Japan. David has either worked with or studied cooperatives in 25 nations.

From 1984 to 1991 he was the National Cooperative Business Association's (NCBA) Director of International Relations and Vice President, Western States. From 1979 to 1985 he was the first Director of Planning for the National Cooperative Bank (NCB) and later was Director of the NCB's Western Region Office.

David is President of the Twin Pines Cooperative Foundation, board member of the Davis Food Co-op and a former board member of Recreational Equipment, Inc., America's largest consumer co-op. In 1995 he was winner of the Consumer Cooperative Management Association's Cooperative Service Award and in 1994 was inducted into the Student Cooperative Hall of Fame.

He is author of Weavers of Dreams:Founders of the Modern Cooperative Movement (1994), co-author of A Day in the Life of Cooperative America and has contributed nearly 200 articles and papers on cooperatives to diverse publications.

Thompson was born in Blackpool, England in the same county as Rochdale – the birthplace of the modern cooperative movement. He has an MA in Urban Planning from the University of California at Los Angeles, where he was given the Dean's Awared for Community Service.

E. G. NADEAU has been working with and studying cooperatives and community development projects ever since his Peace Corps days in Senegal in 1970-71.

He has an undergraduate degree from Harvard University and a Ph.D. in Sociology with a minor in Agricultural Economics from the University of Wisconsin-Madison. He continues to teach courses on an occasional basis at the university.

Dr. Nadeau has dedicated his professional life to research, development and business planning work on cooperatives, community development and employment policy. He was one of the founders of Cooperative Development Services in 1985 and is currently the organization's Director of Research, Planning and Development.

During the past 25 years, he has worked on over 200 cooperative and community development projects.